Dedication

I dedicate this book to the three most hated men on earth.

The rich man who will give away his wealth to the poor.

A man who is wise and shares his wisdom with the ignorant.

The man to whom the Holy Qur'an is revealed.

The gifts of wealth and wisdom combined with the blessing of divine revelation certainly lessened the burden that African Americans continuously endure.

The
African American
Odyssey

Bilal R. Muhammad

authorHOUSE®

AuthorHouse™
1663 Liberty Drive
Bloomington, IN 47403
www.authorhouse.com
Phone: 1-800-839-8640

First published by AuthorHouse   11/08/2011

ISBN: 978-1-4670-3513-2 (sc)
ISBN: 978-1-4670-3512-5 (ebk)

Library of Congress Control Number: 2011916612

Printed in the United States of America

CONTENTS

INTRODUCTION

To Be An African American Man-Child In The Promised Land

The twenty first century is an age of anxiety and restlessness. No doubt a change is imperceptibly overtaking the world. The old order is disintergrating; the new one is however, currently in effect and hastening with rapid speed. And history tells us that such ages of restlessness have also been periods of birth for new movements and cultures. The world is in the grip of a tension and awaits a twenty first century renaissance of man.

Entry into the 21st century has certainly been anything but, what I expected during the excitingly multi-eventful six decades of my life and collectively, that of millions of African American descendents of slaves. The sensationalism of abundant evil and hatred throughout this so-called free and civilized world could either, make a crazy man crazier, or a sane man seek closeness to God and diligently strive to maintain the highest level of human consciousness, I discriminately opted for the later.

The African American Odyssey is not a story about my life as an individual, but a portrait of the African American and a strong compelling history of agonizing convoluted wonderment and events that in many significant ways involved all African Americans, those of the past and the present. However! I was born in and of the adversity that I am herein, projecting and have written about. African American apartheid, segregation and terrorism were a main part of the founding of this country and were clearly prevalent as a familiar part of the environment during my childhood.

I am an African American Muslim with deep Islamic commitments. By this I mean that I am obsessed with confronting the pervasive evil of unjustified oppression, suffering and unnecessary social misery in our world. I am therefore, determined to explore the spiritual intellectual sources and existential resources that feed our courage to be, courage to love humanity and courage to fight for freedom and God given, human rights. I do not identify with the likes of any American political party, though I am currently a registered member of the Independent Party which is for the sole purpose of exercising my voting privilege since I am afforded minimal voting options. I initially thought the Independence party possessed some level of political difference from what already existed only to find that a decade later it had become nearly identical to the prevailing most prominent two political parties and left me once again wondering from which party or position should I cast my votes or should I even vote at all since non-voters in some ways have the real voices that reflect the concerns of the people. I remain un-bias to political party influence as my thinking continuously runs the gamut from pragmatism and revolution through idealism and globalism while the Holy Qur'an and Islam represent the ultimate template and yardstick by which I carefully measure the righteousness and justice of all earthly affairs.

My African American Muslim perspective is put forward in this book which serves as a testament of faith, hope, survival, and sustainability in the twenty-first century.

While writing The African American Odyssey, I've made a conscious and important effort to maintain candor with an appeal to readers who might not be inclined to read at all, or books they regard as repetitious, overly in-depth and dramatically drawn out. I purposefully attempted to avoid monotony and boredom.

During the course of composing this literary work, I kept a statement made by the late great and noble Minister; Malcolm X, in mind, he said; "If you want to hide something from a Black man, put it in a book, he won't read it". The unfortunate truth of that statement certainly resonated in my mind and influenced my initial intent which was to write in a simplistic, fast and easy read, factual and to the point style content that would attract the attention of almost any basic or casual reader and hopefully, ultimately dispel the old conclusive notion of Minister Malcolm's which would certainly be a delight to his spirit and all that he attempted to inspire in his people.

The African American Odyssey is about the timeless heritage of African American people, and a product of the sacred reserve I maintain in my soul, of contrite, great respect and honor for the efforts and traditions of former great African and African American pioneers and leaders, whom with their life blood and strong determination, paved a way for their future generations that would be just a little bit easier. May we never forget the recognition, honor and respect due our beloved ancestors.

I witnessed America's rise to eminent superpower, and the sustainability of her grand empire through the twentieth century. This grand American achievement prompted me to take a close look at my own individual growth, surroundings and journey in life, and has inspired and enabled me to develop a grasp of the complex, conflict ridden dynamics of my African American people and a more flexible perspective on human life in general.

With the mercy and compassion of Allah, I escaped the stigmatized societal dictated limitation cast on African American men, not living beyond their forties. My survival beyond those limitations and obstacles is certainly in no way due to any genius plan and strategy that I drafted and executed, I encountered and fought most if not all the demons and obstacles created for the African American demise and since they didn't totally consume me, I might be considered one of those who managed to slip by, un-noticed, as I knew how to utilize my African American "Invisibility" to my advantage.

Thereafter, I acknowledged that my survival as a Black man in the belly of the beast (America) is for a reason much greater than an individualistic self-absorbed existence, and any extra time extended to me via the grace and mercy of the Almighty God (Allah), should be used conscientiously, constructively and very wisely.

Therefore, the duration of my human existence is henceforth, dedicated to the improvement of my own soul and the much needed fulfillment of the aspirations of my struggling African American people and humanity overall. My spiritual and emotional maturity has produced a clarity within me that has enabled me to see, better understand and appreciate the beautiful yet, injured aching souls of my African American people in ways that I was once blinded to, certainly in part due to the tough facades American society has conditioned us Black people, to wear and act out.

I have begun the duration of my life as a literary artist and social critic desiring to share with those interested, my travels through life as a Black man in America and how I viewed the world through my own set of lenses. Additionally, I intend to work limitlessly, in areas of pro-activity for the advancement of my people, and in hopes that any energy I contribute to our struggles will at the very least minutely lessen our need for excessive dramatic detrimental reaction and close some of the gap between expectation and fulfillment.

I've written this literary work, not as a dramatist, but as a philosophic commentator of African American historical narratives that partake of blood-drenched battles on a tear-soaked terrain in which our lives and deaths are at stake.

The genesis of this book: The African American Odyssey is a literary portrait and chronological record or history about events that were significant to each era of the African American plight that they entailed, an explanation of their causes, a land-mark by which we are directed into the future and a provocation for discussion and pro-action. Many of the events of the African American Odyssey must be viewed in their historic settings; therefore, I attempt to illustrate the African American renaissances with specificity and clarity.

My desire to write about the African American Odyssey was propelled by anguish and what I witnessed to be rapid diminishing enthusiasm amongst African Americans in these most critical of times; which however, is certainly due to the magnitude of African American disparity. Yet! I share the same resentment and difficulty in trying to maintain hope and cautious optimism in the ugly face of evil systemic and institutionalized American white supremacy.

Frightfully concerned for the future and sustainability of my people, I thought it advantageous to distribute through The African American Odyssey, an important reminder of the attention and consideration we must give to time as a premium for African American survival, progression and sustainability.

Many of the events described in The African American Odyssey actually occurred during the span of my life and the most recent of them I must confess, I never in the wildest of my thoughts, dreams and nightmares could have imagined would transpire. With the dramatic recent changes undergone in the world, I actually thought that America could conceivably and possibly ultimately lose her sovereignty, but I never imagined it would be relinquished due to her international debt.

The African American Odyssey is about the millions of Africans abducted and forced into international slavery and how the official ending of that slavery marked the beginning of centuries of evil white American oppression against African American people. It's a historical record entailing the benefits of African American struggle, the exploration of variable new vistas born of necessity, and tradition in the modern world. It's also about the achievements of success by enthusiastic, dedicated African American people for more than four centuries.

The African American Odyssey is an inspirational legacy about former slaves working tirelessly to transform their dreams and aspirations into realities. It's an odyssey entailing the historically significant giant steps African Americans took towards progression which have in recent years unfavorably, converted into giant steps backwards resulting in retrogression and degeneration.

This literary portrait and history gives a depiction of centuries of African American love, prayer and forgiveness for their demonic enemy while maintaining blatant hatred, despise and the ultimate level of contempt for self. I attempt to illustrate from my own perspective how the promise of American democracy came and went, delivering no more than just that, a false and empty promise! The pursuit of happiness, led African Americans to drug and substance induced escapism or social invisibility and numbness.

Invisible Man, 1952, a classic novel by: Ralph Ellison.

"I am an invisible man. No, I am not a spook like those who haunted Edgar Allen Poe; nor am I one of your Hollywood-movie ectoplasms. I am a man of substance, of flesh and bone, fiber and liquids-and I might even be said to poses a mind. I am invisible, understand, simply because people refuse to see me. Like the bodiless heads you see sometimes in circus sideshows, It is as though I have been surrounded by mirrors of hard, distorting glass. When they approach me they see only my surroundings, themselves, or figments of their imagination-in deed, everything and anything except me."

Un-favorable to the African American plight, the African American odyssey with circumstantial critically distracted focus, turned on to a junction of two worlds, belonging to neither, and invisible to both.

While the inherent impetuous hate of African American people continued, fluctuating at one significant period solely due to the distractions of change that the Civil Rights Movement of the 1960s brought. The timely renew ability and resilience of African American people took us from Civil Rights to Black Power as we realized the need to stand as a collective body for the benefit of power and resistance against racist malicious intent in a Euro-American civilization or environment hostile to every aspect of our African American humane existence.

Concern for the souls of African American folk prompt me to issue them a reminder of caution; "once the spirit of the oppressed is broken, the oppressed will usually resign to the acceptance of all forms of oppressive inferior treatment". A people who have been oppressively restricted and held down naturally condescend to the lower levels of delinquency.

As soul starving African Americans unfortunately, increase their development of self destructive passions and ambitions I express in The African American Odyssey, woe's and concern that the toxicity of detrimental elements will repudiate all the hard earned advantageous gains of advancement made by African Americans throughout the centuries.

I attempt to illustrate and present to the reader how the emotional and psychological effects of slavery greatly influenced the events that preceded it.

I further attempt to convey to the reader how the pains of our sufferings and oppressions only hurt us not the oppressor which is in part sufficient reason for African Americans to establish and maintain an un-breakable bond of comradery and affection.

Though I thought and certainly understood America to have a history written in blood, the relevance of Murphy's Law, of "what goes around comes around", and the "Bitch" I grew up being told and understood "pay back" to be, would one day revisit America for "pay back", the bitch had arrived and was demanding "pay back" ("pay back is a bitch") plus interest for default in payment.

I have always ascertained that in the true justice of Allah(God), no one gets away "Scott Free", without accountability for their actions, I just didn't think that during my life time I'd get to see so many of America's "chickens coming home to roost".

As I grew of age I was constantly being encouraged by the elders to wear the world as a loose garment which would enable me to avoid some of the anguish and frustration that could potentially lead to the awaiting madness and hopelessness. I could only wear the world as a loose garment for a short while due to the continuously changing conflicting theatrics of African American life which got tighter in time and inevitably caused me the anguish and humiliation I attempted to avoid.

I never viewed Allah (God) as my co-pilot in the flight of life, in fact I always knew and clearly understood Him to be solely in charge of all of existence, motion, order and law of all things, and I submit to His divine will. "Allah-hu-akbar" (Allah is the greatest). I have therefore, humbly invited Allah to my writing project for assistance and success since it is He that is in charge of all affairs.

I have managed to consciously repulse America's self sufficient, self might, Godless attitude and behavior and I always ascertained that if you practiced effective evil throughout the course of your existence as an individual or a nation, you became an expert at it and that evil inevitably transforms you into an oneness with it.

This I concluded is the clear case and history of America who has created modern terrorism with her extermination of Native Americans and the masterful creation and implementation of international slavery and the evil exploitation of people of color throughout the entire planet.

While researching and writing this book, I looked for grace periods in America's history where she might have taken the opportunity to practice peace weather international or domestic, and there were none.

Ironically, racism is America's oldest and still greatest dilemma and her violations against African Americans continues, and when combined with her previous crimes against humanity, result in un-measured post traumatic injury.

The current overall situation of African American disparity remains an extreme and urgent situation, and extreme situations of this nature require extreme or extraordinary measures!

I pointedly make an attempt to show the reader how the complexities of our unfortunate and disadvantaged position of inferiority in America pose a grave danger to the future survival and sustainability of African Americans. Very much like a devil, America has consistently raised hell all over the planet earth. Of course, I realized that due to specifications in America's initial design, the American system could not work without designated enemies, which consequently also means that America's situations and events will always be confrontational, aggressive and episodically bloody.

America's imperialism and tyranny is based on technologically sophisticated weaponry that can represent a threat to any of America's friends, foes and potential enemies.

America has clearly established that she has permanent interest, but no permanent friends, and only one permanent enemy, the African American.

War and weaponry are two of the most significant aspects of American power.

America has enough nuclear weaponry to dissolve all life forms on the planet several times over and yet she desires more weaponry with hardly any place to store it, and at the very same time pretends to wonder why American youth have such an immense desire and infatuation for guns and thirst to kill other humans.

In this book, I pointedly illustrate the multi-dimensional and multi-faceted aspects of American racism and legalized oppression.

The odyssey of African Americans roamed past the climatic opportunity for revolution and settled for compromise filled with the certainty of despair which should serve as a reminder that our decisions are not made in the hindsight; they're made in the present and should always be made with visionary foresight and consciousness.

I remain concerned with the image the world sees when it looks at the African American and unfortunately, the world views the African American as amusing tragic comic, and pity's them with contempt.

I am therefore, sincerely hopeful that this book, The African American Odyssey, will not only serve as a compilation of African American historical events, but will also serve as a source of intellectual and socio-economic and cultural stimulation for African Americans. I extend that hope to include optimism that this book will additionally serve as a useful handbook of guidance, enabling my grandchildren, future offspring, and particularly the youth of the race to know and understand who I was as an African American Man-Child in the promised land, how I survived the maze of despair, who I have grown into as an elder and literary voice, as well as the thoughts, ideals, principles and convictions I stand on, and how it all transformed into my character which maintains a passionate quest for freedom, justice and equality and an eager desire to urgently replace African American disparity with prosperity and the continual uplifting of my African American people.

I remain on a painful quest for endless wisdom while simultaneously brightening the darkened areas of my soul to create a more mature and compassionate human being.
My socio-political objective of deepening humanity in the world, especially amongst my African American people is a perennial process of highlighting the plight of the wretched of the earth and broadening the scope of human dignity.

The African American Odyssey not only represents the progression of my thoughts and persuasions but also consists of my reflections.

The African American Odyssey will I hope, keep the essential ideas contained within it, alive in the mind of the reader so that they may be debated and refined. I encourage my readers to focus on how they can lead a good and meaningful life-a life in dialogue with history, connected to community-without falling into despair.

This literary work is my feeble attempt to transfigure our African American guttural cry into a call to care-for African American socio-economic, human rights, and political collective causes bigger and grander than our own precious cry.

1.   How the West was won

The United States of America! The World's Premier!

Armed with gun and Bible in hand "Give us what we want or we will destroy you", the relentless words and actions of the Christian European Caucasian White man in his quest to conquer and colonize the West, (America) The New World.

The West or Western World, "America" was a land already occupied by its native inhabitants whom were at the initial point of the White mans invasion called "Indians" a name given to them by the explorer, Columbus who's original intended destination was actually India, thinking he had reached India when first arriving in America.

Much later in American history during the 19th century "American Indians" would be called and known as "Native Americans".

Land Real Estate amongst these natives was certainly not for sale, nor the mere thought of it which sparked aggression in the European White man while occupying and settling on land that he would ultimately forcefully take and colonize.

Upon the White mans arrival in America they knew very little about growing food so with the hospitality of the natives they taught them, particularly the Dutch settlers, to grow and utilize corn a main crop and a variety of other newly acquainted food crops.

The White mans occupation led to his conspired territorial claim while Europeans were migrating to America by the droves with their military forces establishing bases throughout this invaded land. In almost no time the White settlers had become tyrants killing and evicting the natives from their own land with the support and direction of the British Crown (Great Britain) whom these European Whites pledged their allegiance to before establishing an initially intended union in the new world (America).

While the earth reeked of the blood of the massacred Native Americans, white European Colonists settlers desired laborers to help them in the country's development. They turned to Asia and were unable to use the yellow man.

A man named John Hawkins (Plymouth 1532-November 1595). Sir. John Hawkins was an English shipbuilder, navel administrator and commander, merchant, navigator and slave trader; asked permission of Queen Elizabeth of England to take the blacks from Africa into her colonies of America and the West Indies and use them in their development. The Queen asked "what consideration will you give them?"

Hawkins replied "They will be civilized and Christianized in the colonies, for in their own country they are savages and barbarians." Under these pretenses the British Queen signed a charter empowering John Hawkins and others to remove from Africa millions of men, women and children who were sold in the slave markets of the Southern States of America, South America and the West Indies. Parents were separated from children, husbands from wives. All were scattered in the Western Hemisphere to work in the cotton fields of the Southern States of America and the sugar plantations of the West Indies.

The slaves who were sold in the West Indies remained as slaves for two hundred and thirty years and those sold in America for two hundred and fifty years. The West Indian slaves were emancipated by Queen Victoria of England, and the American slaves were emancipated by President Abraham Lincoln.

The first Englishman recorded to have taken slaves from Africa was John Lok, a London trader who, in 1555 brought to England five slaves from Guinea.

In 1800 the population of the United States included 893,602 slaves, of which only 35,505 were in the northern states. Vermont, Pennsylvania, Massachusetts, Rhode Island, Connecticut, New York, and New Jersey provided for the emancipation of their slaves before 1804, most of them by gradual measures. The 3,953,760 slaves at the census of 1860 were in the southern states. West Africa supplied the majority of the slaves that went to work in the Caribbean and America. In the 18th century a long stretch of West African shoreline was called the Gold Coast because of the precious metal that was found there.

Other areas were given names to reflect the materials and resources they had. Next to the Gold Coast there was the Grain Coast and next to that the Ivory Coast. This is still the name of an African country today.

The strip of land in West Africa that used to be called the Gold Coast and the Grain Coast is the location for modern African countries such as Ghana, Togo and Benin. Other countries that supplied slaves were Senegal, Guinea, Sierra Leone, Liberia, Nigeria and Angola.

These and most countries in modern Africa had their borders created during slavery and colonization. New territories were born as a result of the desire for European nations to build an overseas empire. Traditionally these were tribal people-they didn't have, didn't need to have, defined country boundaries. The current country map of Africa is largely the invention of Europeans. This led to the strange divisions of land. For example the French took the West African territory of Senegal but the British claimed its interior and named it Gambia, which is like having Scotland in the middle of England. Senegal, like many countries in Africa, has several ethnic groups with different physical characteristics, cultures, and languages. Senegalese speak Wolof, Mandingue, Toucouleur and Peul as well as French. A few of the many languages spoken in Nigeria include Yoruba, Hausa and Lgbo. English, due to the country's colonial past, is also spoken.

Slave traders became aware of these and other differences. They said that the Mandingoes from Senegal were clever and able to steal the master's goods.

They also said that the Ashanti from the Gold Coast were good workers but likely to stir up rebellion. Slave traders recognized that African people had a wide range of behavior and customs. The African slave trade was sustained primarily by profit hungry elites of all kinds: Christian, Muslim, Jewish, European, Arab, African and American. Yet the distinctive feature of New World slavery was its "racial" character. After a few decades of trans-racial slavery-in which whites, Blacks and reds were owned by whites-this ancient form of subjugation became an exclusively Black and white affair.

Certainly no coincidence to white enslavers that Africa represented the best part of the globe producing the richest of everything from diamonds and rare precious jewels to the rich royal genes of African people. Unfortunately, at this very date, despite the sale and export of their rich natural resources, most African countries such as; Nigeria, known for its oil production and international sale, do not control the economies of their own countries.

Weaponry for Native Americans was initially limited to the manually operated Bow and Arrow, knives and other hand held and throwing weapons until many years later when they were able to acquire guns from the white man. Whites had the advantageous use of the Musket (Riffle) (invented in 1718 by James Puckle) and eventually the cannon which would prove no match for the Native Americans killing them in large numbers.

As natives were being killed off the enslavement of Africans continued to flourish in America. This would mark the beginning of centuries of vicious, murderous and general demonic behavior and attacks by Whites against Native Americans, African Americans and unlimited other races of people of color on Native American soil. These preemptive continuous murderous attacks resulted in the intended extermination of the Native American by Caucasian European invaders.

Native Americans (American Indians) and African American descendants of African American slaves are the only citizens of America that are clearly non-emigrant people.

The Native American, being the natural original inhabitant of the land, and the African American, being abducted from his home and country, and then transported to a strange and foreign land against his will as a slave.

The Trans Atlantic Slave Trade was the enslavement and transportation, primarily of approximately 30 million African people, to colonies of the New World that occurred in and around the Atlantic Ocean. It lasted from the 16th to the 19th centuries. Most enslaved people were shipped from West Africa and Central Africa and taken to North and South America and the West Indies to labor on sugar, coffee, cocoa and cotton plantations, in gold and silver mines, in rice fields, the construction industry, timber, and shipping or in houses to work as servants. The plantation economies of the New World were built solely on slave labor.

America's first real practice, skill sharpening, refinement, and on stage dress rehearsal for becoming the ultimate international tyrant and imperialist power machine was the American Revolution also commonly refereed to as the civil war. Thirteen colonies tired of taxation without representation, the north against the south and the demand for independence from the British. The American Revolution was advocated and encouraged by prominent figures like, Patrick Henry (May 29, 1736-June 6, 1799) served as the post colonial Governor of Virginia and known for his "Give me liberty or give me death" speech. Patrick Henry along with Samuel Adams and Thomas Paine were some of the founding fathers of the United States, advocates of the American Revolution and republicanism. This proved to be the bloodiest revolution ever fought on American soil and was a victory to the Yankees as they defeated the Rebels with the assistance of slaves who would be nominally freed at the end of the Civil War. The war ended in 1865 and slavery was officially abolished that same year though some states had abolished slavery for themselves between 1777 and 1864 and slavery transport from Africa to America was stopped by 1808.

The official end of slavery raised serious concern by Whites of possible revolt from their former slaves which they knew could have potential critical affect as the country was now regrouping from the devastations and casualties of civil war and needed to form and establish a Union (government). African American Slaves oppressively conditioned to maintain their inferiority, for the most part posed no immediate significant threat of retaliation to post war reconstruction. There were however always small fractions of Slaves who were willing to die in their quest and fight for their freedom and that of all slaves. Many slaves journeyed to Canada by walking through the vast Niagara Woods with guidance and direction from Underground Slave Railroad conductors such as Harriet Tubman, Frederick Douglas and William Wells Brown. Numerous slaves successfully crossed the Niagara River though sometimes Underground Railroad passengers, as they were called, were ready to terminate their journey and turn back. Determined Underground Railroad conductors like Harriet Tubman born Araminta Ross 1820 or 1821-March 10, 1913 whom was called the "Moses of her people" escaped to Philadelphia, then immediately returned to rescue her family and slowly one group at a time, she brought relatives out of the state and eventually guided dozens of other slaves to freedom. She carried a little derringer gun and on occasions had to use it to persuade panicked passengers to move on to freedom in Philadelphia, Pennsylvania until the far reaching United States Fugitive Slave Law was passed in 1850 she then helped guide fugitives further north to the freedom the Niagara Falls, Canada slave refuge provided.

A notable few of the many rebel warrior slaves included African American slave ancestors such as Harriet Tubman; an abolitionist who conducted thirteen missions to rescue more than eighty slaves through her underground railroad to freedom.

She later became a Union Spy during the American Civil War and helped John Brown a White abolitionist recruit men for his raid on Harpers Ferry.

Harpers Ferry was the Federal Army raid in which John Brown; accompanied by his two sons who were ultimately killed in the raid, actually seized the army to get the weapons for a planned rebellion by the slaves.

John Brown was hanged for his attempt at starting a slave rebellion and before his death he was asked if he had any last words and he replied, "If I was doing this in the interest or defense of white men, I would be your hero" and then preceded to put the rope around his own neck for his hanging as he had insisted.

There were many White's that assisted in the African American slave plight to freedom and John Brown was the most prominent of them due to his courageous and vigorous challenge to slavery.

On her death bed, Harriet Tubman said "the one thing she regretted was not being with John Brown at Harpers Ferry".

Frederick Douglas (born Frederick Augustus Washington Bailey in 1818-February 20, 1895) is considered the most prominent figure in African American history. Born a slave and after several attempts at freedom escaped and with the education he illegally acquired since slaves were not allowed to be taught to read and write became an American social reformer, orator, writer, statesman and a abolitionist leader advocating freedom. In 1852 Frederick Douglas said, "It is vain that we talk of being men, if we do not the work of men. We must become valuable to society in other departments of industry than those servile ones from which we are rapidly being excluded. We must show that we can do as well as they. When we can build as well as live in houses; when we can make as well as wear shoes; when we can produce as well as consume wheat, corn and rye-then we shall become valuable to society. "Society," continued Douglas "is a hard-hearted affair. With it the helpless may expect no higher dignity than that of paupers. The individual must lay society under obligation to him or society will honor him only as a stranger and sojourner."

Sojourner Truth (Isabella Baumfree) born; a slave in 1797 in upstate NY, Ulster County. Sojourner Truth was born Isabella Baumfree and changed her name giving herself the name Sojourner Truth. She was born on a Dutch settlement and spoke Dutch until she later learned to speak and read standard American English. Unwilling to further endure the persecution and cruel beatings from her slave masters Sojourner Truth eventually escaped slavery by literally walking away from it unsure of the geographical direction of freedom and became an abolitionist. In 1870 she began campaigning for the federal government to provide former slaves with land in the "new west". She pursued this effort for seven years during a century that was anything but kind and considerate of African Americans.

Sojourner's mission and campaign resulted in no success. These are just a few from a long list of countless African American Journey Agents and White's who lived, fought and died for the deliverance of African Americans into freedom. The complexities of the Civil War and mostly post war (Reconstruction Era) left the newly freedom granted slaves without a home or place to live and at this point former slave owners adopted the concept of "Share Cropping". This concept permitted former slaves to stay on the plantations of the former slave masters, work the land and in return for their labor continue to live on the plantation with the oral agreement that the plantation owner reap whatever he desired from the harvest and then give the "Share Croppers" whatever he deemed fit which was often times nothing or vacate notice. Former slaves in their hopelessness and desperation; having no other alternatives agreed with this concept knowing very well it wouldn't be a fair play from the beginning. The factor that kept former slaves humble to these deceitful unfair conditions was destitution, having no possessions or food and no where else for former slave families to go for refuge. Although nominally free, African Americans have never been sufficiently enlightened to see the matter before them other than as slaves. Cases can be cited of African Americans who opposed emancipation and denounced the abolitionists. A few who became free actually re-enslaved themselves. A larger number of slaves made no effort to become free because they did not want to disconnect themselves from their masters, this type of thinking and behavior remains prevalent with African Americans who still object to full freedom.

Since the Civil War when Blacks were first given a chance to participate in the management of their affairs they have been inconsistent and compromising. They have tried to gain one thing on one day by insisting on equality for all, while at the same time endeavoring to gain another point the next day by segregation. At one moment African Americans fight for the principle of democracy, and at the very next moment they barter it away for some temporary advantage. You cannot have freedom or democracy and dispose of it at the same time and not be determined foolish. The ending of the

Civil War and nominal emancipation of slaves marked the beginning of Reconstruction and the evils of Jim Crow, which in turn; provided dreadful significant reason for mass defection of African American former slaves from a cast system in the south.

The Exodus of Blacks from the south was a flight from American terrorism, though, those that joined this mass African American migration had modest expectations. Over a short span of time, and immediately preceding the Civil War, approximately three million African American former slaves making a great leap of faith, migrated to other states mostly north and mid-west.

African slavery sits at the center of the grand epoch of freedom, liberation and equality in the new world. African Americans doings and sufferings remain burdened by the horrific unspeakable memories of the Middle Passage and the chambers of horrors on slave ships. The children of Zion were literally in a strange land and unsuccessfully trying to sing the song of Zion, asking the rhetorical question, "How can I sing the Lord's song in a strange land?"

The most rhythmic people on earth began to harmoniously hum spirited messages into the universe for God to hear, hoping that He would hear their desperate cry and end their unjust agonizing and tormenting oppression.

2.   Seek and Destroy

Praise The Lord And Pass The Ammunition!

Complete domination by way of world wide invasion in the name of Democracy, the pretence of peace and illusion of goodwill is the goal for this new developing nation and all those who oppose its tyrannical imperialist establishing will be killed in the name of freedom, American democracy and the God that the new world declares to have entrusted itself to.

The United States of America was now in her formative years and America's rise to power and eminence would be delivered to her by the use of tyranny in the form of violence, hatred, fear and the gun.
In the preamble of the US Constitution the priority is clearly stated "One Nation under God".
Men like James Madison and Thomas Jefferson were moved by the ideals of Christianity and wanted the United States to reflect those values as a Christian nation however! James Madison was considered by many historians to be an atheist and Thomas Jefferson, an enlightenment-era thinker who rejected the divinity of Jesus Christ and was in France at the time the document was actually written giving little credence to the actual amount of in-depth

sincere righteously spirited soul that went into the creation of these government documents.

The Bill of Rights is really the people's voice against the founding fathers, liberty against conformity. Many of the founding fathers lobbied against the Bill of Rights. Most of them disapproved of giving ordinary citizens freedom of religion, freedom from unreasonable search and torture, the right of free speech and so forth. In fact when John Adams was President (1797-1801) he revoked freedom of speech.

Many of the United States of America's founding fathers were slave owners such as; George Washington (1732-1799) First President of the United States of America and slave owner of many slaves in the state of Virginia. James Madison Jr., (1751-1836) "Father of the Constitution" and fourth president of the United States, slave breeder, importer and owner of many slaves in the state of Virginia.

American history from inception till now has shown that the American founding fathers and Whites in general were never motivated or inspired by truly divine righteous law. America was actually built on the pretenses of moral Christian values.

The right to bear arms was comprehensively inclusive in the US constitution as it was a main and featured instrument in the confiscation of America from its original natives. The Second Amendment to the Constitution of the United States is the part of the Bill of Rights that protects the right to keep and bear arms. It was adopted on December 15, 1791 along with the rest of the Bill of Rights. The gun would ultimately become the world's greatest weapon and instrument of persuasion. With the technological advancements made to guns and general weaponry a single individual could kill countless numbers of people with a flick of a button or press of a trigger. The American media for several decades entertained its audiences with gun fights the first of which was the "Cowboys and Indians". The Cowboys were considered the undisputed good guys and the Indians were considered the savage bad guys, "So much for American history" since now one of the subconsciously main aspects of American culture had become violence and would hence forth till this date in the twenty first century critically intensify. These movies undoubtedly stimulated a desire in most men and boys, young and old to become the most feared and fastest gun in the west. After the invention of the air plane and war ships the American White man eventually acquired the ability to shoot and strike his targets from the sky and waters with his continuous development in advanced technological weaponry. This might and ability to syncopate was transforming the American White man into a "Tyrant Monstrous Power Machine". In order to maintain any acquired power the American White man knew the importance of securing and protecting his ill gotten gains and reestablished the intelligence and skills of his military.

African Americans were limited to the duties they were permitted to perform in the newly reinstituted US Army primarily because they were considered by the White man and government to be less than second class citizens although according to the "Emancipation Proclamation" they were officially "proclaimed" and declared free people. They were only free nominally, according to US constitutional government documentation and by no means considered equal which disqualified them from access to the promise of American democracy and justice.

African Americans never did get the "Forty Acres and A Mule" however, we did get forty plus more years of "pure living hell" in America.

3. Voting Rights Act

African American voter disenfranchisement

Many African Americans are unaware of the historical racist driven obstructive difficulties resulting from their mere desire to exercise their constitutional right to vote, and assume that African Americans didn't begin to vote until the Voting Rights Act of 1965 was passed, when in actuality many African Americans have been exercising their voting rights privilege since their official or nominal emancipation, and other free African Americans voted prior to that emancipation, though, with extreme vicious terrorist deterrence from the Ku Klux Klan and other overall general and systemic American racist hindrance.

The national Voting Rights Act of 1965 was a landmark piece of legislation in the United States that outlawed discriminatory voting practices that had been responsible for the widespread disenfranchisement of African Americans in the United States. Echoing the language of the 15th Amendment, the Act prohibits states from imposing any "voting qualifications or prerequisite to voting, or standard, practice, or procedure—to deny or abridge the right of any citizen of the United States to vote on account of race or color." Specifically, Congress intended the Act to outlaw the practice of requiring otherwise qualified voters to pass literacy tests in order to register to vote, a principal means by which Southern states had prevented African Americans from exercising the franchise. The Act was signed into law by President Lyndon B. Johnson, a Democrat, who had earlier signed the landmark Civil Rights Act of 1964 into law. 1865-1866 Black Codes are passed by southern states, drastically restricting the rights of newly freed slaves. The Fifteenth Amendment to the United States Constitution prohibits each government in the United States from denying a citizen the right to vote on that citizen's "race, color, or previous condition of servitude" (i.e., slavery). It was ratified on February 3, 1870. The Fifteenth Amendment is one of the Reconstruction Amendments. "Section 1. The right of citizens of the United States to vote shall not be denied or abridged by the United States or by any State on account of race, color, or previous condition of servitude. Section 2. The Congress shall have power to enforce this article by appropriate legislation."

The Fifteenth Amendment is the third of the Reconstruction Amendment.
The Amendment prohibits the states and federal government from using a citizen's race (this applies to all races), color or previous status as a slave as voting qualification. The North Carolina Supreme Court upheld this right of free men of color to vote; in response, amendments to the North Carolina Constitution removed the right in 1835. Granting free men of color the right to vote could be seen as giving them the rights of citizens, an argument explicitly made by Justice Curtis's dissent in Dred Scott v. Sandford.

"Of this there can be no doubt. At the time of the ratification of the Articles Of Confederation, all free native-born inhabitants of the States of New Hampshire, Massachusetts, New York, New Jersey and North Carolina, though descended from African slaves, were not only citizens of the States, but such of them as had the other necessary qualifications possessed the franchise of electors, on equal terms with other citizens."

The original House and Senate draft of the amendment said the right to vote and hold office would not be denied or abridged by the States based on race, color or creed. A House-Senate conference committee dropped the office holding guarantee to make ratifications by ¾ of the states easier. The amendment did not establish true universal male suffrage partly because Southern Republicans were reluctant to undermine loyalty tests, which the Reconstruction state governments used to limit the influence of ex-Confederates, and partly because some Northern and Western politicians wished to continue disenfranchisement of non-native Irish and Chinese.

The first African American to vote after the adoption of this amendment was Thomas Mundy Peterson, who cast his ballot in a school board election held in Perth Amboy, New Jersey on March 31, 1870.

On a per capita and absolute basis, more African Americans were elected to public office during the period from 1865 to 1880 than any other time in American history. Although no state elected an African American governor during Reconstruction, a number of state legislatures were effectively under the control of a strong African American caucus. These legislatures brought in programs that are considered part of government's role now but at the time were radical, such as universal public education.

They also set all racially biased laws aside, including anti-miscegenation laws (laws prohibiting interracial marriage). Despite the efforts of groups like the Ku Klux Klan to intimidate African American voters and white Republicans, assurance of federal support for democratically elected southern governments meant that most Republican voters could both vote and rule in confidence. For example, when an all-white mob attempted to take over the interracial government of New Orleans, President Ulysses S. Grant sent in federal troops to restore the elected Mayor. However, after the close election of Rutherford B. Hayes, in order to appease the South, he agreed to withdraw federal troops. He also overlooked rampant fraud and electoral violence in the Deep South, despite several attempts by Republicans to pass laws protecting the rights of African American voters and to punish intimidation. An example of the unwillingness of Congress to take any action at this time is their failure to pass a bill that would have required incidents of violence at polling places to be publicized. Without the restrictions, voting place violence against African Americans and Republicans increased, including instances of murder. Most of this was done without any intervention by law enforcement and often even with their cooperation. By the 1890s, many Southern States had strict voter eligibility laws, including literacy tests and poll taxes. Some States even made it difficult for African Americans to find a place to register to vote.

4. The Discussion

The most massive of storms is brewing on America's horizon and causing instability in the Cockatrice's (legendary serpent with the head of a snake and body of a rooster) ability to continue to fly through the skies with the four ribs of man in its mouth. Needless to say the four ribs represent the Black, Brown, Red and Yellow man.

INJUSTICE APPLIES TO ANY ACT THAT INVOLVES UNFAIRNESS AND HARM TO ANOTHER OR VIOLATION OF HIS OR HER RIGHTS. THE ONLY PROTECTION AGAINST INJUSTICE IN MAN IS POWER-PHYSICAL, SOCIO ECONOMIC AND THECNOLOGICAL EMPOWERMENT.

The African American having been a slave, free labor commodity to the establishment of America stands most distinct, awaiting the gust of winds that will hopefully free them from the yoke of the giant Cockatrice.

African Americans have prayed with intense and assiduous optimism more than four hundred years for divine deliverance from an evil beast that refuses to share with them their earned portion of the American dream. African American sons and daughters of African American slaves have paid with their slave labor and life blood ten fold and far more than their dues and fees for Americanism and a mere share in the American dream and have yet to receive any American Dream product, compensation or refund equivalent to their slave labor investment into an American Dream, instead are continuously severely tormented with an elite version of the American nightmare reserved solely for African American former slaves and their descendants.

Government is: an executive control, a centralized authority for the purpose of expressing the will of the people. Democracy is defined as: a government by the people; rule of the majority, a government in which the supreme power is vested in the people and exercised by them directly or indirectly through a system of representation usually involving periodically held free elections. African Americans were never represented as a free and equal people in the American system and promise of democracy.

Qualification to bear arms in America was determined by the socio economic status of individuals and other non White's which emphatically always spells race, excluding African Americans overall, so much for American constitution, presumptive democracy and its inherent racial preferences and practices. Quite frankly! The origin of gun laws was drafted and intended only to limit the access of guns to African Americans giving white Americans the extra added insurance against any possible retaliatory actions by former slaves and in the event of rebellion incidents, lack of guns would reduce the aggressors might and success. Before the stringency of the gun laws intensified hunters, property owners and privileged others were still allowed the ownership and use of their guns. African Americans during this era and the indefinite future were still the under class and hadn't quite graduated to "second class" yet, but treated as un-official second class citizens with constitutional and civil rights documented into government legislation but unable to exercise and benefit from the privileges afforded them and all American citizens according to the United States Constitution, therefore! Continued to rely on the former slave master to descretionately determine every aspect of their destiny.

Segregation meant clear separation between Collards (Blacks) and whites.

After the Civil War African Americans were referred to officially as Colored, though, they continued to offensively be called with extreme racist evil treatment, hatred and taunt "Niggers". The name or term "Colored" clung to the African American until African American leaders like Elijah Muhammad insisted that African Americans, whom were officially classified by the United States government as Negroes, were "so-called Negroes" and the term "Black" and "Black Man" actively and officially entered the African American vocabulary replacing the word Negro. The question was often asked of white's, why they chose to call the African Americans "Negro", they replied; it was because Negro's were named in honor of the Niger River. Elijah Muhammad sensibly taught Malcolm and his other followers "You don't name people after rivers". "You name people after the land from which they come. Where is the country called 'Negro'?"

Elijah Muhammad preached that African Americans were not really the colored people; he logically explained that the real colored man

21

was the Caucasian white man with the white skin, blue eyes, and blond hair.

He concluded that the original man was the Asiatic Black Man; the father of all civilizations.

Malcolm X emphasized the use of the word "Black" for several years until his scholarly extensive studies and research provided him with a more advanced ethnic identity classification and consciousness to be shared with his African American people.

Separate but equal was a legal doctrine in United States Constitutional Law that justified systems of race segregation and between 1876 and 1965 was commonly known and referred to as **Jim Crow Laws.**

The Jim Crow Laws were state and local laws in the United States enacted between 1876 and 1965. They mandated racial segregation in all public facilities, with supposedly "separate but equal" status for African Americans.

WHITES ONLY!   COLORED SECTION!

Signs that boldly read "Whites Only" and "Colored Section" were every where from water fountains to bathrooms, absolutely everything was segregated. African Americans were always separately restricted and placed in the back which became known and reserved as the "Colored Section".

Under this doctrine services, facilities and public accommodations were allowed to be separated by race, on the condition that the quality of each group's public facilities were (supposedly) to remain equal. The phrase was derived from a Louisiana Law of 1890. Jim Crow in the south meant for example; no matter how slow a white person was driving on the road ahead or beside a Black person, the Black person, by law; could not pass them. There were as many or more un-written rules to Jim Crow as there were written and established Jim Crow laws that African Americans were inhumanely subjected to. Jim Crow was in actuality, the worst imaginable form of American terrorism against African Americans and insured that racism remained the order of the day.

The Fourteenth Amendment of the United States Constitution guaranteed equal protection under the law to all citizens. After the end of reconstruction in 1877 states enacted various laws to undermine the equal treatment of Blacks, Southern states contended that the requirement of equality could be achieved in a manner that kept the races separate. The federal government after reconstruction left the policy of segregation up to the individual states.

The second Morrill Act (Morrill Act of 1890) implicitly accepted the legal concept of separate but equal for the 17 states which had institutionalized segregation. The issue of segregation of public facilities first arose in the context of public transportation not education as many people might think.

A Louisiana law required that whites and blacks ride in separate railroad cars which did not violate the Equal Protection Clause. Later during the peak of the Civil Rights era the noble mother of the Civil Rights movement, Rosa Parks while riding a bus home from a hard days work refused to give her seat to a white woman and move to the back of the bus as was law (Jim Crow) for blacks at that time, ignited a change in American race segregation that couldn't be turned back.

In the midst of the Civil Rights era, the prominent phrase; "Keep Your Eyes on the Prize", derived as a reminder to African Americans of what the struggle and movement was about and what the ultimate goals were. "Keep Your Eyes on the Prize", was originally a folk song that became influential during the civil rights movement. Although it was composed as a hymn well before World War I, the lyrics to this version were written by civil rights activists Alice Wine in 1956. It is based on the traditional song, "Gospel Plow", also known as "Hold On". There were many undocumented instances involving African Americans like that of Rosa Parks but unfortunately they didn't get the support or exposure from African American communities usually discriminately due to social and economic factors in their backgrounds.

African Americans even amidst these trying and racially challenging times were usually selectively looking for superficial qualities such as; skin complexion, education, religious connection, and even economic community status of Blacks before validating and choosing their particular "fight for freedom" battles.

The well known "House Negro v. Field Negro" "Willie Lynch" mentality definitely carried over from slavery and unfortunately remained an important class feature among African Americans and light skin African Americans are still prevalently preferred, more privileged and featured in the newness of the 21st century, over darker skinned African Americans. This four century old practice is still regularly practiced and the prevailing unfortunate mind set of Blacks and the advantageous controlled benefit of Whites.

Prior to the era's of the civil rights movement light skinned African Americans commonly engaged in what was known as "Passing" a term that meant an African American individual was light enough in complexion to pass for white which was the criterion for acceptance into most general areas of American and African American society such as, colleges, social organizations, entertainment and certain employment opportunities. Probably the most well known case of segregated education is the Brown v. the Board of Education, Topeka

1954. Linda Brown an eight year old African American girl denied permission to attend a school five blocks from where she lived in Topeka, Kansas, assigning her instead to a segregated school for Black children 21 blocks from her home. Linda Brown's parents filed a lawsuit to force the schools to admit her to the nearby, but segregated school for white children.

In 1954 The Supreme Court ordered immediate integration upon the victory of Brown v. Board of Education and the court concluded that segregated schools were inherently unequal. Brutality against African Americans had already become a prelude of American racism systemically built into America's cultural, social, economic and political infrastructure as a direct result of slavery.

African Americans began to flex themselves defensively with an aggression that would be targeted and executed on other African Americans and not their oppressor, perpetually because of an inherently instilled fear that the slave masters psychologically embedded in them during the early stages of slavery. They were taught to despise each other for any number of superficial reasons such as house Negro, verses field Negro, lighter skinned, verses darker and many other "Willie Lynch" tactical enslavement strategies.

The **"Willie Lynch"** speech is an address delivered by Willie Lynch to a white audience on the bank of the James River in Virginia in 1712 regarding control of African American slaves within the colony. The letter is a verbatim account of a short speech given by a slave owner, in which he explains to other slave masters that he has discovered the "secret" to controlling African American slaves by setting them against one another.

Willie Lynch was the master of a "modest plantation" in the British West Indies who was summoned to the Virginia colony by local slave owners to advise them on problems they were having in managing their slaves.

He suggested that slave masters adopt his technique of exploiting differences such as age, and skin color in order to pit slaves against each other instead of the violent method of handling unruly slaves which was lynching. Some historians speculate the name Lynch as the source of the word "Lynching."

There are some African American historians of African American Studies that dispute the actual existence of Willie Lynch and the events associated with him, however, the reality of the events associated with Willie Lynch became un-disputable realities and are sadly as prevalent today as they were during the actual days of slavery.

The present American system under the control of whites trains the African American to emulate, love and desire to be white and at the same time convinces them of the impropriety or the impossibility of becoming white. African Americans are as critically displeased with their God made natural features and imagery as they were in their days of chattel bondage that changed their rich and royal ancient cultural conditioning. Lighter skin, keen features and what has become known as good hair are the unfortunate epitome of African and African American beauty. Probably the most self hated natural feature that African Americans possess is their natural hair type and second to that is their resentful dark skin color.

Not all, but it might be regretfully accurate to say that most African American women, more so than men would do almost anything to have the hair type of the Caucasian people whose imagery they've emulated and adored for centuries. The intensity of this inferiority issue being more dominant among African American women as opposed to men is to some extent, attributed to the mere fact that woman overall naturally exhibit their hair as a sign of femininity and beauty of which white woman have set the world's standard in modern civilization causing African American women particularly, and women of color a continuous image challenge.

"Black Hair" as it's commonly called, has produced an inherent physiological "displeasure infection" in African American people which directly connects to their ruptured race identification or "Fractured Identity" issues. Many African Americans view their skin color as the symbol of the ultimate curse of God.

To handicap Black people by teaching them that their Black face is a curse and that their struggle to change their condition is hopeless is the worst sort of lynching. It kills the aspirations in a people and dooms them to vagabondage, crime, and unlimited despair.

Having their names and absolute identities totally taken away upon enslavement left African American slaves almost clueless as to who they were, where they came from and what purpose they served in the earth other than that of abject slavery.

Their names, language and their God, was taken away from them when they arrived in America which was the second significant step towards breaking their African free spirit, the first step was their abduction.

The original people of the earth have always traditionally named themselves with attributes of the creator until coming to the shores of America as slaves where those names were taken away and replaced with names of the European slave master who assumed names of the creation since he knew very little to nothing about the creator.

The drudgeries and persecutions enslaved African Americans had to endure left them with what sociologist and psychologist refer to as a "Fractured Identity". Fractured Identity is basically defined as; "If who you think you are is at odds with who you actually are and as a result your functioning in society is impaired". Classified examples include multiple personality disorder and a brain containing two identities with each only knowing of itself. These examples are clearly symptomatic in the issue of ethnic, social and cultural identification of the African American to the level of acute identity crisis.

The dysfunctional existence of African American people in America has always been severely impaired largely due to the White Euro-American racist fanning of Anti-African American sentiment. All African American slaves were forbidden to play any type of drums; hindering them from transmitting messages of revolt or escape to other slaves instead they resorted to sending messages through gospel music and slave work songs.

The very first privilege African Americans were given while enslaved in America, was the right to sing gospel. They were granted this right even before being allowed the right to learn to read the Gospel or read at all.

The question about teaching slaves to read and write remained a dilemma throughout the entire slave period. The slave master knew that to teach the slave to read and write he might ultimately emerge as a thinker. These thinkers would inevitably question whether they should be slaves or eventually try to become free.

As African American slaves hewed out melodic, rhythmic inspirational expressions in song, whites mocked and ridiculed their sounds and concluded that the African slave was moaning and grunting and this peculiar aspect of their behavior was typical of them foremost; because African's didn't have souls and additionally due to their non-human, "savagery" which caused their inability to communicate like civilized humans.

In time this perception by whites drastically changed with the superior quality of sound that was produced by African Americans in every music type imaginable from Gospel and Rhythm and Blues to Jazz, Rock and Roll, Soul Music and on to Rap. The superlative and unique artistry of African American musicians throughout the centuries could really never be duplicated despite numerous attempts by countless white artists who made attempts to emulate them.

The gospel voice of Mahalia Jackson became one of the most influential voices in the world especially when she sang "How I Got Over" in 1963 at the March on Washington in front of 250,000 people.

Muddy Watters, considered the "Father of Blues" influenced R &B, Jazz, Rock and Roll and other music styles. Undoubtedly! Jazz is the highest of all music forms and the voice and soul of African American people.

Miles Davis and John Coltrane were two of music history's extensive list of the most prominent and certainly outstanding Jazz and music artist extraordinaire. To know and understand the spirituality and brilliance of John Coltrane, you must know a "Love Supreme" which was an ode to Coltrane's deep faith and Supreme love for God.

Yet to appreciate the magnificent talent and message of conviction and hope felt in the music of Miles Davis, you had to know that "Some Day My Prince Will Come" and "Kind of Blue".

Miles Davis was one of the most innovative, influential and respected figures in the history of music and the most widely recognized jazz musician of his era, an outspoken social critic and an arbiter of style-in attitude and fashion-as well as music. His album "Kind Of Blue" is the best-selling album in the history of jazz music and was praised by the United States House of Representatives to "pass a symbolic resolution honoring the masterpiece and reaffirming jazz as a national treasure."

Little Richard dreadfully journeyed several decades before finally receiving the accolades and recognition he deserved for actually being the creator of Rock and Roll.

The incomparable dynamics of Jackie Wilson was the first to incorporate dance with singing and was the initial reason for Berry Gordy's vision and establishment of Motown Records and Jackie Wilson gave Motown Records their very first hit.

Rap music shares a history that many rap artist of today might not even be aware of. Rapping actually refers to "spoken or chanted rhyming lyrics." The art form can be broken down into different components or separated into "content", "flow" (rhythm and rhyme), and "delivery".

Rapping is performed in time to a beat. Rapping is a primary ingredient to hip hop music, but the phenomenon predates hip hop culture by centuries.

Rapping can be delivered over a beat or without accompaniment. Stylistically, rap occupies a gray area among speech prose, poetry, and song.

The use of the word to describe quick speech or repartee long predates the musical form, meaning originally "to hit". The word had been used in British English since the 16th century, and specifically meaning "to say" since the 18th. It was part of the African American dialect of English in the 1960s meaning "to converse", and very soon after that in its present usage as a term denoting the musical style. Today, the terms "rap" and "rapping" are so closely associated with hip hop music that many use the terms interchangeably. Rap etymologically means "fast reed" or "spoken fast".

It may be from a shortening of repartee. Rapping can be traced back to its African roots. Centuries before hip hop music existed, the griots of West Africa were delivering stories rhythmically, over drums and sparse instrumentation.

Unfortunately, in recent decades rap music has transformed into amusing tragic comic and significantly different from the blues, which is also amusing tragic comic.

The main components that clearly distinguish rap from the blues are its petulant and profane violent lyrics, misogyny of woman and cavalier use of the "N" word (nigger). These distinctions make most rap music tragic toxic comic that amusingly reflects by glorification of negativity and mockery, all the ills and disparities of African American life.

Comedy and the very best of it usually derive from tragedy, pain and conflict. People who do comedy well do tragedy well, which is the clear case and point of African Americans whom the world finds amusement in their misery. When delivering their comedy, African Americans find comfort and confidence in acting out the circumstances or behaviors of someone other than themselves that they share some emotional identity or similitude with.

Another classic example of amusing tragic comic is when stand up comedians greet the women in their audience, saying; "good evening bitches! Women whose names I don't know I respectfully call them bitches". The tragedy here is the clear replicated reality of how Black women are perceived by the world and disrespectfully treated by Black men.

African American women find a tragic comfort in being referred to as "bitches" by Black men, and experience casual comfort in referring to themselves as "bitches".

For centuries whites couldn't comprehend the universal rhythm that the African American possessed quite simply because they didn't have rhythm or soul but in time they grew to understand that music had sustaining and redeeming power for the African American.

Since their emergence from the caves and hill sides of Europe the nature and behavior of Europeans became more sterile and clinical as they were learning basic human behaviors like; walking upright, not eating their deceased, properly disposing of their waste, burying their dead, preparing their food and practicing the very basic aspects of general human behavior which would prepare them to enter civilization and adopt an entry level of human culture. During this particular time in what would be considered ancient history or the history of mankind; Caucasians were the newest humans to civilization and were eating their dead, clueless to how to dispose of their waste. Prior to this particular beginning period in their civilized development, Caucasians would inhabit caves and lay in-coupled with dogs which provided them with body heat and from this is where the European's bestiality, extreme love and excessive fondness of the dog derived. Since Caucasians were already weak in flesh, blood and bone they easily contracted additional diseases from the dog then transmitted those diseases to humans of color as they migrated exploring the wonders of the earth.

Their initial travels and explorations quite often resulted in communicable toxicity, spreading their infectious small pox, common cold, and other diseases which rapidly killed numerous natives of various parts of the world. As a result of some degree of their canine connected history and inherent race hate, American Caucasian's express more consideration, love, and fondness for what they consider to be their canine companions, than they do for fellow African American human beings.

If one didn't know better you'd think whites were the creator's of Jazz because of the emphasis they put on this particular music form above and beyond all others and despite the fact that Jazz was once considered the devil's music by white's and the sound of it wasn't allowed in their homes. For centuries whites have said that rhythm was a sin.

Every African American has the right to sing the "blues". "The same old fight, you know you can't win, this is where the blues begins".

True "blues" are expressions of the oppressions and atrocities lived out by African Americans on a daily basis, so the "blues" is as old as the African Americans existence in America and every African American knows how to sing the "blues", the "blues" ain't taught, the "blues" is natural, un-intended, un-rehearsed and when African Americans are not focused they know they become susceptible to catching the "blues".

The "blues" will come to you wherever you're at, you don't have to go looking for the "blues". You can have the "Harlem Blues" or the

"Watts Blues", the "Georgia Blues" or the "Mississippi God damn blues", the blues travels everywhere just like bad news or gossip. African Americans above and beyond anyone else, are experts at detecting individuals with the "blues", they even know the "blues from a distance and when its own its way. The "blues" was for centuries reserved as a normalcy for African Americans but in later years the white man's got true severe cases of the "blues". The most unique thing about the "blues" is that "the blues don't care who get em" because "true blues aint never no good new news".

No doubt! The "blues" is profoundly tragic-comic. A good and welcomed indication of things getting better is when the "blues" start delightfully turning green.

Whites exert themselves in trying to emulate those very same moans and groans only to find that the expressions of the African American are and have always been naturally in tune with the universal and divine order of things and not against that natural motion or order.

When African slaves arrived in America they brought with them religious traditions many of which immediately began to dissipate. The pain and drudgery of slavery drove them to seek meaning and hope in a new place-the Bible of which they did not know that while Euro-American enslavers were enacting slavery on Africans in the New World (America), in 1611 King James hired the most brilliant writers in Europe, including William Shakespeare, Francis Bacon, and Christopher Marlowe, to rewrite the Bible.

The Authorized Version, commonly known as the King James Version, the King James Bible or simply the KJV, is an English translation by the Church of England of the Christian Bible begun in 1604 and completed in 1611. First printed by the King's Printer, Robert Baker, this was the third such official translation into English; the first having been the Great Bible commissioned by the Church of England in the reign of King Henry VIII, and the second having been the Bishop's Bible of 1568. In January 1604, King James I of England convened the Hampton Court Conference where a new English version was conceived in response to the perceived problems of the earlier translations as detected by the Puritans, a faction within the Church of England. James gave translators instructions intended to guarantee the new version would conform to the ecclesiology and reflect the Episcopal structure of the Church of England and its beliefs about an ordained clergy. The translation was by 47 scholars all of whom were members of the Church of England and included prominent notables such as; William Shakespeare, Francis Bacon and Christopher Marlowe. James VI was king of Scots from 24th July 1567. On 24th March 1603, he also became King of England and Ireland as James I when he inherited the English and Irish crown and thereby united the crown of the Kingdom of Scotland with the crown of the kingdom of England and Ireland, each remained legally separate though ruled by James. James continued to rule until his death in 1625.

One area of the life of King James that for many years remained clouded in controversy was allegations that James was homosexual. As James did father several children by Anne of Denmark, it is actually more accurate to say that he was allegedly a bi-sexual. While his close relationship with a number of men were noted, earlier historians questioned their sexual nature, however, few modern historians cast any doubt on the king's bisexuality and the fact that his sexuality and choice of male partners both as King of Scotland then later in London as King of England were the subject of gossip from the city taverns to the privy Council. His relationship as a teenager with fellow teenager Esme Stuart, Earl of Lennox was criticized by Scottish Church leaders, who were part of a conspiracy to keep the young king and the young French courtier apart, as the relationship was improper to say the least. Lennox, facing threats of death, was forced to leave Scotland.

When James inherited the English throne from Queen Elizabeth I in 1603, it was openly joked that: James is now Queen!

It should also be noted that George Villiers, also held an intimate relationship with King James, about which King James himself was quite open. King James died in 1625 of gout and senility.

Though most slaves couldn't read, biblical stories of salvation and retribution spread among them rapidly and approximately sixty five years into slavery African American slaves were allowed to become Christians with stipulated limitations.

This was the first time in human history a collective race of slave people would accept their slave masters God and religion. Israel's enslavement to Egypt under the rule of the Pharaoh's didn't convert them to the worship of Pharaoh's multiple God's, and Moses immediately returned to his God, religion and people upon learning of his birth right.

EXODUS 1446 BC, The time that the sons of Israel lived in Egypt was four hundred and thirty years and the Lord led the people by way of the wilderness to the Red Sea.

Another reflection of the African American's struggle to "Exodus" through the wilderness of America a bondage that's lasted more than four hundred years with a lingering hope to find "ZION", the city of David, the promised land and God's dwelling place with his people.

African Americans dramatically crossed the religious divide in search of hope, acceptance, and inspiration in Christianity and the Bible. Even upon becoming Christian worshipers of the slave masters God and practitioners of his religion, African Americans still didn't receive admiration, courtesy nor basic civil human treatment by their white American Christian counterparts. When John Hawkins went to Queen Elizabeth of England, requesting her permission to abduct and enslave Africans to be brought to her colonies for labor, Queen Elizabeth asked him what consideration he was going to give these slaves, and he replied; "they will be Christianized and civilized as they are savages in their own land".

As a child and product of the Civil Rights era which entailed continuous pro-active movements such as Elijah Muhammad's Nation of Islam, Marcus Garvey's Back to Africa Movement, and The Black Panther Party of Self Defense. On several occasions I distinctly recall hearing many Black folks respond to the galvanizing calls of leaders like Elijah Muhammad, Marcus Garvey, and most Black leadership in general by saying; "the white man did us a favor by bringing us out of Africa, we were over there running around with plates in our lips and bones in our noses like savages."

These and similar statements made during that time were typical to hear and have apparently become inherent in the decedents of African slaves.

In more recent years I've heard African Americans and African Caribbean's express that the white man gave them Jesus. I was initially taken back by the words simply because I knew that this type of thinking was prevalent but didn't think the feelings could be so enthusiastically verbally expressed which left me wondering if my African American people remained Christianized today due in part to a sense of obligation and indebtedness owed to the former slave master and his children for transforming savage Africans into civilized Christians which was the consideration John Hawkins assured Queen Elizabeth the slaves would be given when taken into her colonies in the Americas and the West Indies.

In schools of theology African Americans are taught the interpretation of the Bible worked out by those who have justified African American oppression and winked at the economic debasement of the African American sometimes almost to the point of starvation. Deriving their sense of right from this type of teaching, graduates of such schools can have no message to grip the people whom they have been ill trained to serve.

Europeans just concluded during the voyages of Columbus which was just a few centuries ago, that the earth was actually round and not flat, which prompts me to beg to differ with whomever might think that Europeans qualify to administer religious, spiritual, and civilization guidance. Their newness to the world has not given them the sufficient time or experience to evolve in the world as humanly conscious beings and they certainly know little to nothing about the spiritual nature of the universe which causes them to implement various forms of evil and destruction with minutely limited sensitivity and little remorse. For this reason when studying history as it is offered in the American school system from elementary school throughout the university level, you would never hear Africa mentioned except in the negative. You would never thereby learn that Africans first domesticated the sheep, goat, and cow, developed the idea of trial by jury, produced the first stringed instruments, and gave the world its greatest boon in the discovery of iron. These schools and universities would never inform or teach that prior to the Mohammedan invasion about 1000 A.D. these natives in the heart of Africa had developed powerful kingdoms which were later organized as the Song hay Empire on the order of that of the Romans and boasting of similar grandeur.

Inasmuch as I continuously advocate and campaign for African American reparations, I am sadly reminded that the outcome of such a campaign has already been decided against by those African Americans chained and shackled by psychological debt obligations to the former slave master and his children. Far too many African Americans view and regard the issue of reparations with a stoic point of view or with little to no importance primarily due to their inherently imbedded psychological feelings of indebtedness to whites for Christianizing them and rescuing them from what they, the former slave and slave master, considered to be African savagery while the truth to this equation is that African Americans were forcefully made subjects to the Euro-Christian religion just as they were to Americanism.

These two aspects, (civilizing/Christianizing and reverse indebtedness) of the multiple personality disorders that the African American experiences is clear and explicit of how African Americans can love and pray for their enemy, and further explains with psycho-social behavioral evidence that the white man isn't an enemy to African American Christians at all, but is instead their very best friend. The issue of African American reparations therefore, poses extreme challenge and enormous doubt as does the overall plight of the African American masses, yet for many African Americans particularly those of the Christian persuasion, if the issue never arises again it would be sufficient and gratified mainly due to the subconscious reverse and everlasting indebtedness African Americans feel towards whites for delivering their salvation and which also serves as negligible hindrance to the potential of any campaign movement for reparations for the horrific enslavement of African Americans. The Christian religion that has been extended to the descendant's of African slaves is merely a loan from whites who have enslaved and segregated Africans, and African Americans; and most Black Christian based organizations, though to some nominal degree are independent, are clearly dominated by the thought of the oppressor of African American people.

Consequently, the white man could be further assured of their superiority and the Black man could be made to feel that he had always been a failure and that the subjection of his will to some other race is necessary for the freedom, yet, he would then still be a slave. If you can control a mans thinking you do not have to worry about his action. When you determine what a man shall think you do not have to concern yourself about what he will do. If you make a man feel that he is inferior, you do not have to compel him to accept an inferior status, because he will seek it himself.

If you make a man think that he is justly an outcast, you do not have to order him to the back door. He will go without being told; and if there is no back door, his very nature will demand one.

During slavery one of the many effective techniques used to control and oppressively condition slaves was fear.

The eminent threat and routine implementation of slaves being sold and separated from family easily broke their spirit and instilled the most inherently inhumane type of fear in generations of them.

The fear of a mother having her child taken away from her and sold is the most unimaginable horrific atrocity inflicted by human beings who would set the standard and lead the way for civilization in the modern world.

The sale and separation of slaves made them agreeable to everything the slave master willed, though, the separations/sales occurred anyway by the authorization of slave masters in spite of their empty promises, guarantee, or good word.

Blacks today, fear whites just as they did centuries ago and are complicit to their blatant and subliminal demands and experience anxieties caused by not knowing and understanding the racist and evilly vicious modern forms of entrapment for African American neutralization, family separation, and destruction in such forms as; Crack, AIDS, Prison-industrial complex and murder.

Because of the African American conflicted conscious and in some cases subconscious reverse indebtedness to the former slave masters for delivering them from savagery and Christianizing them, the African American's concept of freedom, justice and equality have been severely compromised and therefore, limited to whatever extent the former slave master's children permit.

Several decades ago my mother and I, engaged in an in-depth discussion which entailed both of us asking the million dollar question, "What caused the African demise, decline and deviation so far away from world leadership to become the most inferior race on earth".

Our speculations led us to objectively re-examine ancient African history, of which we concluded that Africans overall had become extremely pagan which enabled European invasive entry, race mixing, their exploitation of differences, and ultimately familiar pagan practices in America that would include everything from the worship of man and the sun to the worship of money.

It's no wonder why African Americans ran into these Euro-Christian pagan practices precipitately, they sensed something familiar in it as did the people who became impatient with Moses and built for worship, the Golden Calf.

African American people, descendents of slaves would then evolve in America to become the most hated, despised and rejected people ever on earth even after their expressions of worship in some cases, love and adoration for their former slave master and his children.

Every other group of people, Blacks included, would find perpetual reason to despise the African American even foreign Africans residing in the African continent shun, scorn and ridicule the African American with feelings of superiority over them and ironically the word and term "Nigger" would only apply and historically cling to African Americans and not Africans of other nations throughout the globe. Here is where we also find that the African American has failed to recover from his slavish habit of berating his own and worshiping others as perfect beings. Effective propaganda techniques implemented by White Americans throughout the past centuries distanced all other Blacks of geographical variations from African Americans and suggested a superiority complex among them that would enhance the international Black divide and conquer. The vehement hatred that the White man has been successful at mustering up amongst other ethnic groups throughout the world and against

African Americans has held African Americans in a vulnerable and stagnant position.

THE ENTIRE WORLD HAS STOOD IDLY BY AND WATCHED THE SUFFERING OF AFRICAN AMERICAN PEOPLE.

African Americans are for certain, an endangered people subject to murder by an American oppressive racist government regime and society that has been inherently groomed to despise, persecute and exterminate their very existence.

Late great visionary Black leaders such as Marcus Garvey and Elijah Muhammad, like David with only a rock in his hand, courageously attempted to slay the oppressive evils of a racist white American Goliath trying strenuously to encourage and establish African American Business, trade and commerce having seen first hand the urgent essential need for Blacks to produce food, clothing, education and shelter for themselves. Marcus Mosiah Garvey, Jr. Founder and leader of the "Back to Africa" movement, Born in Jamaica West Indies August 17, 1887 was believed to have been mysteriously poisoned on a ship and died June 10, 1940.

Marcus Garvey was a Black Nationalist and Pan Africanist founder of the UNIA (United Negro Improvement Association) and inspired a global mass movement focusing on Africa. The UNIA was referred to and known as an African movement of Redemption. Mr. Garvey becomes known for his famous slogan; "One God, One Aim, One Destiny.

Marcus Garvey's campaign insisted that Africa was for the Africans and European Colonial powers immediately exit Africa. The US government grew extremely concerned with the positive and constructive impression Mr. Garvey's progressive movement was making on people of African decent and oppressed people of color, across the globe. During the 1920s Mr. Garvey became friends with a young Vietnamese seaman named Ho Chi Minh, who regularly attended UNIA meetings during his brief stay in New York. The rapid growth and continuous progress of Marcus Garvey's Back to Africa movement with his fleet of ships, "The Black Star Line" prompted the government to go to work on discrediting the practices and imagery of Mr. Garvey by first lambasting him and his global African empowerment philosophy and once again with the assistance of solicited Black sell-outs the government ultimately dismantled his global movement. When Mr. Garvey arrived in America and visited the office of the NAACP (National Association for the Advancement of "Colored" People) to interview Mr. W.E.B. Du Bois, who at that time was regarded as the leader of the "Negro" people and who had recently visited the West Indies, Mr. Garvey was dumbfounded on approach to the office to find that but for a Mr. Dill, Mr. Du Bois, himself and the office boy, he couldn't tell whether he was in a white office or that of the NAACP. The entire staff was either white or very near white, and thus Mr. Garvey got his first shock of what he considered the advancement of hypocrisy. There was clearly no representation of the African American race there that could be recognized.

The advancement meant that you had to be as near white as possible, otherwise there was no place for you as stenographer, clerk or attendant in the office of the NAACP. After a short talk with Mr.

Du Bois, Mr. Garvey became disgusted with him and his principles then suddenly the thought he never contemplated entered his mind, which was for him to remain in America to teach Mr. Du Bois and his organization what real race pride meant. When Mr. Garvey left the office of the NAACP to travel about the nation to study the social life of the African American he found that the light skinned complexion policy of the NAACP was well observed in business, entertainment, education, professional life and other aspects, all over the country.

In restaurants, drug stores and offices all over the nation where African Americans were engaged in business it was discoverable that those employed were the very "lightest" members of the race. Mr. Garvey asked "What's the matter? Why were no black, brown-skin and mulatto girls employed? And he was told it was "for the good of the trade. This certainly put a strain on the relationship between Mr. Garvey and Mr. Du Bois the negative effects of which would revisit them both in the years to come. William Edward Burghardt Du Bois (February 23, 1868-August 27, 1963) was an intellectual leader in the United States as a sociologist, historian, civil rights activist, Pan-Africanist, author, and editor. Born in Great Barrington, Massachusetts, Du Bois graduated from Harvard, where he earned his PhD in History, the first African American to earn a doctorate at Harvard. As head of the National Association for the Advancement of Colored People (NAACP) in 1910, he was founder and editor of the NAACP's journal The Crisis. Du Bois rose to national attention in his opposition of Booker T. Washington's alleged ideas of accommodation with Jim Crow separation between whites and Blacks and disfranchisement of Blacks in the south, campaigning instead for increased political representation for Blacks in order to guarantee civil rights, and the formation of Black elite who would work for the progress of the African American race. After more than ninety years of un-wavering devotion to African American freedom, W.E.B. Du Bois left America for Africa and concluded: "I just cannot take any more of this country's treatment. We leave for Ghana October 5th and set no date for return . . . Chin up and fight on, but realize that American Negroes can't win." In the end, Du Bois's views of American optimism failed him. He honored the invitation to Ghana, extended to him in 1961 by Ghanaian President: Kwame Nkrumah, and not very long after died in Accra, Ghana in 1963 at the age of ninety five. In his treasured book titled "The Souls of Black Folk," when reflecting on Alexander Crummel, the famed African American cleric and African nationalist, W.E.B. Du Bois wrote, "Three temptations he met on those dark dunes that lay gray and dismal before the wonder-eyes of the child: the temptation of hate, that stood out against the red dawn; the temptation of despair, that darkened noonday; and the temptation of doubt, that ever steals along with twilight." Hate, despair and doubt are serious temptations that cause dire consequences and havoc. Du Bois very clearly understood the danger and destructiveness of despair and said it was that which "darkens noonday."

Indelible spiritual remnants of historical pioneering leadership like that of W.E.B. Du Bois, The Honorable Marcus Garvey, The Honorable Elijah Muhammad, Martin Luther King Jr. and Malcolm X, remain deep in the hearts and minds of African people in America and throughout the world. In this twenty first century Blacks still don't have an economic infrastructure despite the efforts and examples of previous Black leaders such as Marcus Garvey and Elijah Muhammad. These visionary men sought to establish farms, banks, transportation and other essential industries for the proliferation of African American people.

THERE IS NO RACE OF PEOPLE ON EARTH SO JUST AS TO GIVE OTHERS, FOR THE ASKING, A SQUARE DEAL IN THINGS ECONOMIC, POLITICAL AND SOCIAL.

African Americans first occupation in America was farming and may become extinct for African Americans. For sure, American farmers of all races have decreased in number over the years, but none as dramatically as African American, who now comprises only 1 percent of the nation's nearly two million farmers, according to U.S. Census figures. At the turn of the century African Americans owned 20 million acres of land and now own only 3 million acres. There are currently only 80 thousand African American farmers in 42 states.

The sad reality for African Americans collectively is that they don't own or have their own, "The house we're in is burning down and the White man aint coming to save us".

America spends billions of dollars on international humanitarian aid yet ignores the starvation and deteriorating conditions of American human beings right at home.

African Americans are classified quite differently from other Americans and people of foreign nationalities which are reflective in America's response to any major disasters involving Blacks such as Hurricane Katrina.

Hurricane Katrina of the 2005 Atlantic hurricane season was the costliest natural disaster, as well as one of the deadliest hurricanes, in the history of the United States, claiming the lives of 1,836 people.

African Americans are an endangered people on many fronts as they routinely run, ducking and dodging the death devices designed and continuously upgraded by a fascist so-called democratic government and society for their immediate eradication or ultimate demise. The African American is an obvious moving target enemy to a White American redundantly racist society, its government, law enforcement agencies of every level and the repetitious Black against Black crime instilled in African Americans for the purpose of maintaining manipulating control of them through their political and socio-economic unrest.

Given the national crime statistics and actual facts disfavoring Blacks it is absolutely imperative that African Americans exercise their constitutional right to possess fire arms (Guns) for the defense and protection of their persons, families and property. African Americans should and must as all other American persons protect and defend themselves at all cost, self defense being the ultimate.
African Americans are statistically disproportionately the main victims of murders and various other crimes though often times perpetrated by other African Americans due to the ill effects of racist, unjust, disenfranchised, disillusioned, societal perpetuation. They tend to be the constant victims of tragic deaths resulting from police brutalities and excessive force. African Americans have unfortunately inherited the pathetic position of exclusivity with epidemics such as MURDER, AIDS and CRACK.
The prevalence of racism in America permeates today as intensely as it did before and during the civil rights era, the only difference is the change of dressing and the facial facade creating a more colorful and pretentious illusion nonetheless the game of racist hate and evil

remains the very same. In recent decades the African American has not had the privilege of real substance sincere and dedicated leadership, just superficial political representation and the masses of African American people have always accepted the intentions and actions of the statesmen and leaders of other races as being directed in their interest as a group in conjunction with the interest of others.

Such a feeling on the part of African Americans caused them to believe that the constitution of the United States was written for African Americans, as well as the Constitutions of countries such as, England, France, Italy, Germany and other countries where African Americans have their present domicile, as citizens or subjects. The clear fact that African Americans oppressively suffer today under whatever flag they reside is proof positive that constitutions and laws, when framed by the early advocates of human liberty, never included and were never intended for African Americans as human beings. It is by sheer accident that African Americans happen to be fellow citizens today with the descendants of those who, through their advocacy, laid the foundation for Human Rights. This means that African Americans overall can expect very little or nothing from the efforts of present day leaders of other races.

The African American resumes walking about in the wilderness of America disillusioned, disenfranchised and like Lazarus in the Biblical scriptures continuing to beg the rich man for the crumbs that fall from his table. Though African Americans have assimilated into American culture and exhausted every conceivable plea for freedom, justice and equality they remain the bitter victims of American political, social and economical repression. In this near end, year of 2010 African Americans are asking the repetitive question, "What do we do now?" The answer and solution is simplistic yet repetitive like the question, African Americans in their quest for resolve and socio-economic empowerment must absolutely once and for all times right now and in the immediate future become a collective force, which automatically equals power and the power is sufficient for effective pro-action and significant achievements in progress.

Power prevails as the only argument that satisfies man. African Americans must take the risk of disposing of their hindering differences and join an "African American Race Collective" that seeks and desires only its sole purpose which is the inanimate objective of power which is convertible into socio-economic access. African Americans must take full control and direction of their own dollars as well as demand access to some of the billions of dollars they generate into the American economy.

African Americans can no longer afford to allow Euro-American Caucasian Jews and other outsiders to guide and direct their dollars away from the benefit of their own African American people and communities.

They must grasp hold of the economics and politics of their communities insuring that their children and elders get all the essentials needed to sustain themselves.

African Americans must establish and put in place the necessary institutions that will shape, mold and fashion Black youth into tomorrows promise of successful socio-economic advancements and sustainability.

African American communities must emphatically empower their young adults to become courageous, accountable and responsible leaders to themselves, society, their families and their communities. The African American must immediately learn to educate, feed, clothe shelter and provide all basic essentials for themselves and their community.

If the African American in the ghetto must eternally be fed by the hand that pushes them into the ghetto, they will never become strong enough to get out of the ghetto or its disparities. It becomes frightful to think of the consequences African Americans would additionally endure as a result of further procrastinating, ignoring or shunning the realities of the new requirements and demands of a new global order of current and future socio-economic adjustments and futuristic matrix existence.

The hardships and drudgeries of day to day survival for African Americans has unfortunately blurred their vision causing them to loose sight of the "Prize" they were encouraged to keep their eyes on and disabling them to see and understand the current matrix era the world has entered before the turn of the 21st century. Lack of preparedness for the matrix era causes hindrance in the global community.

Matrix is a rectangular array of mathematical elements (as the coefficient of simultaneous linear equations) that can be combined to form sums and products with similar arrays having an appropriate number of rows and columns, an array of circuit elements for performing specific functions, and a main clause that contains a subordinate clause. It is absolutely imperative that African Americans become a collective and solid content for socio-economic empowerment and new order of things.

Bilal R. Muhammad

"Whenever you hear a man saying he wants freedom, but in the next breath he is going to tell you what he won't do to get it . . . he doesn't believe in freedom."

Malcolm X

5.   Black Power

Power concedes nothing without demand
Marcus Garvey

This was the beginning of another challenging unjust and demanding era in the African American struggle and plight with bitter and extremely active persecution of Blacks by a nation so profusely hateful they would go to any length and extreme to undermine and dissolve the existence of African American people.

African Americans had already proven beyond any challenge or doubt that they were indeed the best athletes in the world, which gave Blacks a much needed greater sense of self esteem and beginners place of recognition in the modern world of sports and entertainment. Significant achievements in sports and entertainment by African Americans created in them, a more intense desire for human recognition, social equality and an end to all forms of racial injustice.

Entry into the world of entertainment for African Americans demanded of them that they present their talent in a ragged comedic manner until classically sophisticated and natural talented Men like the late great Paul Robeson came along to defy previous perceptions of Black buffoonery. Paul Robeson; born Paul Leroy Robeson (April 9, 1898-January 23, 1976) was an African American bass-baritone concert singer, recording artist, athlete and actor who became noted for his political radicalism and activism in the civil rights movement. He was the son of an escaped slave, Robeson was the first major concert star to popularize the performance of the Negro spirituals and was the first Black actor of the 20th century to portray Shakespeare's Othello on Broadway. A nationally renowned football player from 1917 to the early 1920s, Robeson was an all-American athlete, Phi Beta Kappa Society laureate during his years at Rutgers University. In 1923 he drifted into amateur theater work and within a decade he had become an international star of stage, screen, radio and film.

James Earl Jones, Sidney Poi tier and Harry Belafonte have cited Robeson's lead film roles as being the first to display dignity for Black actors and pride in African heritage though one of the most internationally famous people of the 20th century, blacklisting during the Cold War has largely kept Paul Robeson out of the mainstream interpretations of history. At the height of his career, Paul Robeson chooses to become a political artist whose hard work and efforts in the struggle for human rights, particularly those of African Americans, actually inspired the career of Malcolm X. Malcolm considered Paul Robeson his hero and adopted his oratory style from regularly listening to Paul Robeson's radio talk show. Paul Robeson's tenacity, poise, and articulation compelled Malcolm's admiration. Mr. Robeson argued that it would be very foolish for African Americans to fight their Asian brothers. He urged Blacks to resist being drafted for the Korean conflict. Robeson said that African Americans "know that if we don't stop our armed adventures in Korea today, tomorrow it will be Africa . . . I have said it before" Robeson continued, "and say it again, that the place for the Negro people to fight for their freedom is here at home. Paul Robeson was also responsible for creating and organizing the campaign to awaken the "sleeping giant", Africa. He was an outspoken advocate of Africa's liberation since the early 1930s. As president of the Council on African Affairs, Robeson had traveled around the world pushing for an end to apartheid in South Africa and to colonialism elsewhere on the vast African continent. In 1950, Robeson's passport was revoked under the McCarran Act over his work in the anti-imperialism movement and what the U.S. State Department called Robeson's frequent criticism while abroad of the treatment of Blacks in the U.S.

Under heavy and daily surveillance by the F.B.I. and the C.I.A. and publicly condemned for his beliefs, Robeson became nearly a non-person. Robeson's right to travel was restored in 1958 and his already faltering health broke down under controversial circumstances in 1963. He was forced into permanent retirement. He would spend his final years in seclusion, unapologetic about his political views and career.

Jack Johnson, born: John Arthur ("Jack") Johnson (March 31, 1878-June 10, 1946), nicknamed the Galveston Giant", was an American boxer, the first African American world heavyweight boxing champion (1908-1915). He was trained in the art of pugilism by Joe Choynski, who also became his friend and sparring partner. Johnson was born in Galveston, Texas. He was born to parents who were former slaves. Johnson's defeat of James J. Jeffries in 1910 caused Whites to riot across the country while Blacks were jubilant over his victory. In some areas of the country police interrupted several attempted lynchings. Riots occurred in more than 25 states and 50 cities. About 23 Blacks and 2 Whites died in the riots and hundreds more were injured.

Josephine Baker; born: Freda Josephine McDonald (June 3, 1906-April 12, 1975) in St. Louis, Missouri, was an American-born French dancer, singer, and actress. Baker was the first African American female to star in a major motion picture and to integrate an American concert hall, and to become a world-famous entertainer. She is also noted for her contributions to the Civil Rights Movement in the United States.

Don Barksdale, born; Donald Angelo Barksdale in Oakland, California (March 31, 1923-March 8, 1993) was a professional basketball player and a pioneer with a number of African American first to his credit.

Bobo Brazil, born; Houston Harris (July 10, 1923-January 20, 1998) was an American professional wrestler, better known by his ring name, Bobo Brazil. He is credited with breaking down barriers of racial segregation in professional wrestling. Harris is considered one of the first successful African American professional wrestlers, and is often referred to as "the Jackie Robinson of professional wresting".

Jackie Robinson, born; in Cairo, Georgia, Jack Rosevelt "Jackie" Robinson (January 31, 1919-October 24, 1972) was the first Black Major League Baseball (MLB) player of the modern era. Robinson broke the baseball color line when he debuted with the Brooklyn Dodgers in 1947. As the first Black man to play in the major leagues since the 1880s, he was instrumental in bringing an end to racial segregation in professional baseball, which had relegated Black players to the Negro leagues for six decades. The example of his character and unquestionable talent challenged the traditional basis of segregation, which then marked many other aspects of American life, and contributed significantly, to the Civil Rights Movement.

These and other African American achievements paved the way for Blacks to be able to exhibit their masterful and superlative abilities to the dismaying disbelief of white America and the entire world. The hard work and efforts of our early African American pioneers and surrogates represent examples of great courage and fortitude.

The Nation of Islam and the Black Panther Party had become influential power forces in African America and African Americans proudly sought through the inspiration of these movements to improve their degraded conditions through education, cultural continuity and more importantly unity.

These two organizations placed strong emphases on the African Americans basic need for self improvement by way of collective economic development, ability and right for Black people to protect and defend them selves. Most African American organizations during this faze of what was known as the civil rights era were eager for integration, satisfied with eventually being able to go to the bathroom with White folks and eat at the same restaurant counter with them and here was a man and organization, Elijah Muhammad demanding reparations for African Americans and teaching them the true identity of the original man.

Elijah Muhammad; born, Robert Poole in Sandersville, Georgia October 7, 1897 and died February 25, 1975. Elijah Muhammad was the founder and leader of the Nation of Islam, declared to have met with God in person (Master Fard Muhammad) whom taught Elijah Muhammad for three years all that he needed to know to build the Nation of Islam. Elijah Muhammad was responsible for the rare and unusual teaching of the original man and reverse philosophy of white supremacy, teaching African Americans that the White man was actually a grafted man from the weak gene in the Black man and the devil in person, commissioned to literally raise hell all over the planet earth for a stipulated period of time and incapable of doing any good. His teachings slightly similar to that of Noble Drew Ali founder of the Moorish Science Temple, and inspired also by the work and philosophy of Marcus Garvey, was quite persuasive attracting millions of African Americans from every state in the country to the Nation of Islam. Intensely concerned with the vicious legacy of American institutionalized racism and hatred of African Americans, Elijah Muhammad requested land from the United States government, eight to ten states and additionally insisted that African Americans be tax exempt.

These demands and others by Mr. Muhammad and the Nation of Islam made everything else that African American organizations of that era asked for look small and damn near insignificant.

ANY RACE OF PEOPLE THAT IS WITHOUT AUTHORITY AND POWER, IS A RACE WITHOUT DIGNITY AND RESPECT.

The Nation of Islam under the leadership of its founder and teacher "Elijah Muhammad" was according to FBI documents, perceived to be the most threatening African American movement to the government's manipulating control of African Americans due to their tight knitted militarily religious, nationalist organization and strict discipline.

Mr. Muhammad insisted that the Black Man in America must be resurrected from the dead level and be taught the true knowledge of himself and others. The Nation of Islam changed the image and behavior of African American men and woman immediately dressing them in suit, ties and maxi length dresses until the recruits earned acceptance into the F.O.I. (Fruit of Islam) and M.G.T. (Muslim Girl Trainee) at which time they became inducted, given their X, which replaced their slave name, (last name) and militarily uniformed.

Induction into either of these units meant more than a simplistic basic membership and required its adherents to enhance their daily quality of life, educational and social skills. Elijah Muhammad called African Americans to the Nation of Islam from every condition and walk of life, ironically the first to adhere to his call were the most destitute, impoverished and rejected among African Americans and eventually the teachings of Mr. Muhammad attracted even the most privileged, talented and gifted.

Elijah Muhammad preached that God was a black man and for the first time in America, this concept made African Americans feel a unique inspiration, rejuvenation and hope having a God that looked like themselves and one that they could certainly identify with.

This reverse philosophical and psychological imagery concept however, proved problematic for many African Americans who inherently felt inferior to whites and dismissively repulsed the whole notion of a black God associated to any religion.

These are the African Americans that are easily identified when images of a white Jesus and Moses are put before them, they consciously and sub-consciously accept its authenticity, but when presented with black images of the very same, they usually passionately comment that "God has no color", yet in the core of their minds and hearts they still visualize God and all things divinely associated to God, white in image and regard the subject as offensive and a provocative desecration.

The substance of the argument is replacing a white idle with a black idle, while the most significant factor should be, particularly in the case of Jesus, the Gospel that he brought and the intended message contained within it. The initial incentive for many of the adherents to the Nation of Islam was establishing autonomy, a Black nation, economic empowerment and the "Do for self" and "Love thy self" philosophy. This organization was responsible for the cultivation and production of brilliant minds, talent and great leadership of people such as Malcolm X, Muhammad Ali, Minister Louis Farrakhan and an endless list of many others. It was the inherently cultural creativity of brothers from the Nation of Islam and other Black Power movements during the nineteen sixties that the word "Rap" was re-introduced and became a very popular phrase among African Americans with a connotation that simply meant; Gift of gab. Initially when a Black man(a Brother) stood and articulately talked to his people about remedying the ills of African American disparity and oppression or encouraging unity and culture the brother was considered Raping. In no time the phrase became common reference to any group of Black people talking, they were "Raping about something" or raping to a chick. The word rap began to be used in the same context as years later in 2000 "Hollering" was the trend word, like hollering at a honey. By nineteen seventy Rap became poetic expression of African American revolution for the purpose of freedom, justice and empowerment.

The Nation of Islam is to a large extent responsible for the general spread of the religion of Islam in America particularly when Warwith Deen Muhammad (Son of Elijah Muhammad) assumed leadership of the organization preceding his father's death in 1975 leading millions of the adherents to "Suni Islam" or traditional Islam as he had many years prior, become a practicing Suni Muslim himself and excommunicated from the Nation of Islam by his father for his difference in Islamic belief and spiritual ambitions.

Warwith Deen Muhammad (also known as Wallace D. Muhammad) was the person that informed Malcolm X of the allegations and scandals that had begun to leak regarding his father's (Elijah Muhammad) indiscretions, impregnating a number of the young sisters in the Nation of Islam including, Sister: Evelyn Williams a former fiancée of Malcolm's whom he had been romantically involved with for several years prior to his membership with the Nation of Islam, were indeed true and caused Malcolm to become agonized and perplexed. This marked the beginning of a chain of unpleasantly hateful power struggling events between Elijah Muhammad, his protégé, Malcolm X and the influential power pushers at the Nation of Islam's headquarters in Chicago. Malcolm intuitively knew that his escalating bitter differences with the Nation of Islam would be resolved with death and violence.

Malcolm X was assassinated February 21, 1965 at the Audubon Ball Room in Harlem, New York while speaking before a live audience. Though tumultuous disagreement, constant antagonism and numerous attempts on the life of Malcolm, his family and close followers indirectly connect Elijah Muhammad to attempts on the life of Minister Malcolm by way of his fanatically emotional devout followers who would have done absolutely anything for their charismatic leader and teacher, Malcolm insisted that whoever was working for his demise was not working alone but was being assisted by local N.Y.P.D. police and federal government agents who trailed Malcolm's every movement during his tenure with Elijah Muhammad and certainly in the final years of his life and strategically exploited for their advantage, the incendiary differences between Elijah Muhammad and Malcolm X.

Prior to Malcolm's excommunication from the Nation of Islam, Elijah Muhammad herald Malcolm X and considered him to be his most dedicated follower and star pupil national representative, this status and influence eventually caused internal jealousy and strife among some of the ranking members and a significant membership split within the Nation of Islam resulting in Malcolm's excommunication from the Nation of which many followers eventually accompanied him in his exit. Malcolm X, sought to expand his horizon at this drastically eventful point in his life and career, by traveling throughout the African continent and the Middle Eastern part of the Muslim world to perform the obligatory Hajj (pilgrimage to Mecca), obtain a long desired knowledge of Africa and the world of Islam and form African American alliances with Africans and the darker people of the world. During his second trip to Africa Malcolm was overwhelmingly accepted as Africa's long lost son. He took his plan of bringing the United States government before the United Nations over human rights violations, with him and began to circulate a memorandum, calling upon newly independent African nations to condemn the United States for its violations of Black human rights. He argued that "Racism in America is the same that it is in South Africa."

"THE BALLOT OR THE BULLET", a speech delivered by Malcolm X, April 12th, 1964 in Detroit, Michigan marked the beginning of an encouraging and inspiring political enlightening period for African Americans and Minister Malcolm X, and a clear indication that he had become independent of Elijah Muhammad's teachings and leadership and was from this point forward, his own man with a revised Black Nationalist agenda.

In his brilliant speech, Malcolm X described how potent a weapon the ballot could be, if it was exercised with care. He expressed that "a ballot is like a bullet. You don't throw or cast your ballots until you see a target, and if that target is not within your reach, keep your ballot in your pocket". Although he advocated exercising the ballot, Malcolm expressed skepticism that voting would bring about full equality for African Americans.

The government, he said, "is responsible for the oppression and exploitation and degradation of Black people in this country. This government has failed the Negro". According to Malcolm, one of the ways that the government had "failed the Negro" was its unwillingness to enforce the law. He pointed out that the Supreme Court had outlawed segregation, "which means a segregationist is breaking the law". But, he said, the police departments and local government often side with segregationist against the civil rights movement. Malcolm said that relying on the federal government to force local governments to obey civil rights laws was futile. "When you take your case to Washington, D.C., you're taking it to the criminal who's responsible; it's like running from the wolf to the fox. They're all in cahoots together".

Malcolm insisted on elevating the struggle of African Americans from one of civil rights to one of human rights.

A fight for civil rights is a domestic matter, and "no one from the outside world can speak out in your behalf as long as your struggle is a civil-rights struggle.

Malcolm said that changing the fight for African American equality to a human rights issue changed it from a domestic problem to an international matter that could be heard by the United Nations.

This speech was a very clear indication of how vast the scope of Malcolm's horizon had expanded and it would now pose a new challenge to state that he had actually grown wiser than any man in the world during that period. His simplistic breakdown of the American political process was delivered with a captivating poise easy for everyone's comprehension.

Malcolm's Black Nationalist Movement was now in full force without the influences, constraints, arbitrary commands or overtones of Elijah Muhammad and the Nation of Islam which once restricted him. Not long before Malcolm's death, he was recognized as the most legitimate African American Muslim leader to the international African and Muslim world. Many · in the African American communities had already been introduced to a more orthodox version of Islam than that of Elijah Muhammad's Nation of Islam.

Sheikh Al-Hajj Daoud Ahmad Faisal, one of American Muslim's unsung hero's was born in 1891 purportedly on the Caribbean island of Grenada. He came to the United States as a young man and in 1920 married an African American woman named Khadijah. Over the years she became a dutiful aid to his Islamic work. Their combined efforts ranged from the founding of the Islamic Propagation Center of America in 1928 (at 143 State Street in Brooklyn, NY) to the establishment of a commune known as the Madinah Al-Salaam near Fishkill, New York in 1934 (which lasted until 1943). Many of African America's Muslims came by way of what was commonly called; State Street Mosque, including, myself, the author. Sheikh

Daoud was quite instrumental from his Islamic space and quarters at State Street Mosque and his official appointment to the United Nations, in raising the level of human rights particularly amongst African Americans going as far back as the mid-1920s.

The Ahmadiyya Muslims were known for opposition to legal segregation, Jim Crow, and actually produced the first African American Muslim permitted a visa to perform the Hajj (obligatory Muslim pilgrimage to the Holy City of Mecca). Ahmadiyya Muslim Community (also referred to as the Ahmadiyya Muslim Jama'at or simply Jam'at Ahmadiyya), was founded in 1889 in India by Mirza Ghulam Ahmad of Qadian (1835-1908. The original movement split into two factions soon after the death of the founder. Racism amongst American Christians led many African American artists, writers, and intellectuals in the 1940's and 1950's to consider converting to Islam. Significant converts to Islam and the Ahmadiyya movement during that era included: Bill Evans, who changed his name to Yusef Lateef; Kenney Clarke (Liagat Ali Salaam), Art Blakey, Ahmad Jamal, McCoy Tyner, Dakota Staton, John Coltrane, Dizzy Gillespie and an extensive list of many more.

No doubt! The religion of Islam became a very significant part of the African American religious experience and particularly from the significantly eventful popularity of the Nation of Islam and Malcolm X; the religion of Islam was growing rapidly among African Americans.

The mere untimely death of Malcolm X caused African Americans to take a look at and examine the teachings of Elijah Muhammad and traditional Sunni or orthodox Islam as it became the practicing tradition of Malcolm X and many of his followers after his disconnection from the Nation of Islam. Malcolm appealed to a broad range of Africans and African Americans, from various walks of life though not all were Muslims. Malcolm X, is clearly representative of an African Americans chance to become the "somebody" America denied them the provisions and opportunity to achieve. He emphatically encouraged Black people to maintain integrity and convictions by standing firmly on principles that are right and benefit the entire race. Malcolm issued a constant reminder to his people that "if you don't stand for something, you'll fall for anything". From this point forward, Islam was no longer considered to be a strange and foreign word and religion to African Americans.

A mind that remains in the present atmosphere never undergoes sufficient development to experience what is commonly known as thinking.

No African American thus submerged in the ghetto, will have a clear conception of the present status of the Black race or sufficient foresight to plan for the future; and they drift so far toward compromise that they lose moral courage.

POWER TO THE PEOPLE!!! RIGHT ON!!!

By this time, all across America chants of "Power to the people" and "Right On" could be heard in every Black community. These chants and phrases were the signatures of the mighty and courageous Black Panther Party for Self Defense.

The Black Panther Party for Self-Defense as it was originally known was founded by: Bobby Seale and Co founder: Huey

P. Newton October 15, 1966 was active in the United States from the mid 1960s-1970s came into existence and as a result of community activism in Oakland, California initially setting forth a doctrine calling primarily for the protection of African American neighborhoods from police brutality.

Police brutality against African Americans was common practice throughout the country and African Americans in cities like Oakland, California became fed up with the police brutalities that replaced the common KKK lynching and cross burning in the south and took action against it.

They decided it was time to organize a self defense movement that would defensively resist the brutality and basically police the police, monitoring their behavior and movements within the black community of Oakland, California.

The Black Panther Party for Self-Defense eventually blossomed and in no time spread throughout the country as did the Nation of Islam and though the Nation of Islam's members didn't visibly bear fire arms the Black Panther Party thoroughly researched, interpreted and public ally exercised their constitutional Second Amendment right.

The Black Panther Party like the Nation of Islam attracted some of the most brilliant people and minds in African America. Angela Davis, Stokley Carmichael, Joanne Chesimard, Eldridge Cleaver, H. Rap Brown and an endless list of many others were dedicated soldiers in the party and adopted "Essays of Chairman Mao Zedong" (The little red book) as a protocol for the Black Panther party's movement and understanding the principles and practical application of communism and revolution. They were considered an African American revolutionary left-wing organization working for the self defense of black people. This philosophy and practice caused fear of mayhem with White's all over the nation. White's had grown extremely concerned that a group of African Americans had adopted and fostered the "eye for eye", "tooth for tooth" and "life for life" concept of justice previously advocated by Malcolm X, created a contrived hysteria in White America.

All Black Power movements in America were considered subordinates to US power and a threat to white racist American Imperial ambitions. The FBI having both of these groups under constant surveillance began to take extreme measures and direct action against the Black Panther Party in an effort to relinquish it by infiltration, agent provocateurs and the use of internal dissidents which precipitated and ultimately failed.

The FBI then antagonized, provoked, obscurely created and then engaged in out and out police combat situations with this organization and was intrigued by the intense dedication African Americans had to this and other liberating African American organizations.

African Americans everywhere in the country were feeling rejuvenated and were exercising their God given inherent sense of loyalty to themselves and the struggle for freedom, justice and equality. The FBI, CIA, (Government) concluded it was time to tranquilize and anesthetize the African American communities throughout America with drugs the benefits of which would be marginalization, civilian manipulated control by government and monetary profit to stimulate the economy. The FBI under the directorship and dictatorship of J. Edgar Hoover, determined that African American organizations of these similitude's are never to foster, exist and thrive in America again, issuing a classified bureau directive to his agents that the leaders of these particular two and inclusive other organizations were to be immediately neutralized, Malcolm X being at the top and priority number one on that list.

Malcolm X occupying as he does an iconic and most prominent place in African American history deserves the importance he has been accorded. He was the most advanced visionary African American leader of his time. Minister Malcolm X perceived that integration was one of the worst institutions for African Americans leading them to retrogression and ultimately degeneration and decay.

Malcolm X planned to submit a petition to the United Nations stating in part that "The Black Mans problem of racism and oppression is a human rights violation and constituted an international problem and therefore! Should be bought before the World Court" (United Nations General Assembly) for international resolve.

The United Nations General Assembly is the main deliberative, policymaking and representative organ of the United Nations. It comprises all 192 Members of the United Nations. It provides a unique forum for multilateral discussion of the full spectrum of international issues covered by the Charter. The Assembly meets in regular session intensively from September to December each year, and thereafter as required. All members of the United Nations are represented in the General Assembly. Each nation, rich or poor, large or small, has one vote.

Malcolm X told African Americans that their freedom by any means was necessary and was disturbed by the racist trickery of the American government to promote the sale and use of drugs, alcohol and gambling items then locking African Americans up for being intoxicated and gambling. It is because of Malcolm X that African Americans discontinued the use of the words and classifications "Negro" and Black with his creation and leadership of the OAAU

(Organization of African American Unity) established in 1964 which in addition to combating injustice also informed Black People that their true identity is African.

OF ALL OUR STUDIES, HISTORY IS BEST QUALIFIED
TO REWARD OUR RESEARCH.

Malcolm X

Malcolm's brilliance and genius led him to continue on the road for African American advancement which had been previously paved by greats like Marcus Garvey with a global agenda. Malcolm X in the twentieth century exposed the African American to awareness and enlightenment of the African continent and people, and encouraged alliance with Africans everywhere in the world with Africa and African America as movement bases and focal points. Because of his tenacious ability to convey to African Americans, the ways in which American government actually worked and how they might grow politically mature enough to understand and manipulate those systems, was of major concern to the government and increased the danger that threatened Malcolm's life.

From time to time rare great people like Malcolm X (EL Hajj Malik Shabazz), are born and other intuitive people that enhance their ideologies with their un-hesitant support like the true dedicated and sincere brothers and sisters that soldiered side by side with Minister Malcolm, recognizing the rare brilliant leadership he contained, and loyally dedicated themselves to his progressive movements. For African Americans, Malcolm X was for a certainty, our Black Shinning Prince and extraordinary example of a real man, and leader that stood on principle and unselfishly accepted that he had a debt and responsibility to history.

Despite Malcolm's differences with Elijah Muhammad and the Nation of Islam, Malcolm refused the many retaliatory offers of support to violently engage followers on either side of the dispute in a potentially bloody war; he was un-selfish and concerned for the lives of all his people to his very end. His life came to an abrupt end when some foolish Blackman was influenced to think that he would be doing God or the government a favor, by shooting Malcolm down, like he was some wild dog in the night.

When I think of Malcolm's assassination, I hear the voice of his close aid and loyal friend, brother; Earl Grant, who in an interview with Gil Noble, the host of "Like It Is", expressed how he witnessed the man at the scene of Malcolm's murder, and immediately determined to be the assassinating shooter, being beat, kicked and stomped and he never let out a moan. My common sense suspicion, however far fetched it might sound to some, tells me he was drug induced or perhaps under the mind control of the F.B.I., by something similar to that of the "Manchurian Candidate".

Undoubtedly! The setup had its sophistications that rendered itself un-noticeable yet quite advanced for the 1960s and although differences between Malcolm X, Elijah Muhammad and the Nation of Islam were volatile, witnesses to the events of Malcolm's assassination unanimously agree that it was an operation clearly successfully carried out by a combination of law enforcement operatives of the N.Y.P.D. and F.B.I. agencies. The N.Y.P.D. and F.B.I. knew that Malcolm's destiny was assigned for assassination.

When I left the Bureau we employed over three hundred full-time informants who reported from allover the country. Most of them were involved in crimes like hijacking, bank robbery, murder and kidnapping. But some were members of the Black Muslims, the Black Panthers . . .

> William C. Sullivan,
>
> key FBI official who spearheaded
>
> COINTELPRO against black activists

"COINTELPRO" against Black activists.

"COINTELPRO" acronym for counterintelligence programs, COINTELPRO is a series of FBI counterintelligence programs designed to neutralize political dissidents. This intelligence program actually began when singer and actress; Eartha Kitt, offended President Lyndon B. Johnson's wife during a White House dinner although Ms. Kitt was one of the many people, targeted by the FBI with no particular political bent.

COINTELPRO was in full operation making every effort with the solicited and recruited Black sell out informants willing to sacrifice fellow African Americans on the alter of a racist oppressive American regime and needed to bring down groups considered to be "Communist Front Organizations" which included all African American organizations and a list of less significant others.

Unfortunately there were some African Americans that willingly collaborated in the J. Edgar Hoover witch-hunt.

These two particular organizational movements, the Nation of Islam and the Black Panther Party proved to be very progressive thereby attracting the dedication and memberships of African Americans throughout the country by the millions.

COINTELPRO ultimately effectively killed most Black Panther Party leaders, imprisoned some and sent others into exile. Because of their persistent demands of justice and readily self defense, the Black Panther Party was feared and reluctantly respected by White America.

After the assassination of Malcolm X, Martin Luther King knew that his time was drawing near and he would more than likely be the next of America's sacrificial Black Shepard's, and with reasonable concern, expressed to his African American people; "It won't be long now", which refers to the victory of civil rights, and his death which he knew would be the price for his honest hard work and victory earned by the collective blood drenched efforts of Black people in America.

Because of the assassination manner in which Malcolm X was killed prior to Martin, many of his immediate aids and supporters physically distanced themselves in hopes to avoid being killed in the line of fire intended for Dr. King.

Dr. Martin Luther King Jr. born (January 15, 1929-April 4, 1968) he was actually born Michael Luther King, Jr. but later changed his name to Martin. He became the most revered African American leader due to his non violence approach which some African Americans viewed as pacifist in principle and at age 35 was awarded the Nobel Peace Prize. Dr. Martin Luther King Jr. is probably best known for his most brilliant "I Have a Dream" speech and his inspiring "Letter from a Birmingham Jail", which was a manifesto of the Negro revolution. Dr. King's African American leadership career was inspired in large part by the efforts of SNCC (Student Non Violent Coordinating Committee) which was a group of African American students attending Shaw University in North Carolina, refused service at a Woolworth lunch counter which led to sit INS at Woolworth lunch counters all over the south by African American college students. Dr. King was a formally educated clergyman impressed and influenced with the philosophy and teachings of Mahatma Gandhi.

During the civil rights era most of America grew to validate Dr. King as the most recognized, valid and ultimate leader for African American people due to his nonviolent philosophy. This philosophy and approach appeased the government and Whites only for a short while.

Precipitately the sentiments of Dr. King's philosophy and movement eventually changed due to the inevitable political and racially tense climate the civil rights movement was creating as many African Americans concluded that the non violent approach worked only up to a certain point then conversion to fighting fire with fire become adopted and applicable.

This is when many African Americans actually began thinking and talking "revolution" instead of nonviolence and Dr. King's publicly expressed views on the Vietnam War which were not favorable to American government and changed the image of Dr. King in the eyes of many white Americans that began to consider him a communist.

Before the death of Malcolm X and Martin Luther King Jr. the two African American leaders cordially formed a cohesive alliance for the purpose of human rights and the potential progression for African American people.

In past but recent decades, I've repeatedly heard African Americans say that Dr. Martin Luther King Jr., died for his people, but Malcolm X would be the uncompromised voice that African Americans would have to listen to and learn from.

Dr. Martin Luther King Jr. was an example of the positive impact one person could have on an entire nation. I, like many African Americans remain convinced that Malcolm X would hold the leadership position on African American politics if he were alive today.

Black action networks and power based movements have begun to die down leaving blacks vulnerable to the tricks of white American cutthroat racist politics.

African Americans have no current authentic African American leadership, only African American local representation and representatives with greater American political ambitions.

Almost all of the current African American representation is without African American accountability and transparency, which in part means that they have transformed into a resemblance of the very same politically oppressive entity that African Americans are fighting and resisting. Like many other African American representatives, they exploit the disparities of African Americans which enable their political careers to blossom and advance for their individual prestige and financial gains.

Like Elijah Muhammad and Malcolm X, many African Americans clearly understand the vicious powers of American institutionalized racism and therefore, are not surprised by its delivery and effect and have no unreasonable expectations of Americanism beyond what her history has thus far presented.

If the saying hold's true; "you judge a tree by the fruit it bears", it would then be un-reasonable to expect otherwise.

I must honestly confess that I am one of many African Americans who are suspicious of racist white America and have very little or no confidence at all in America's falsely proclaimed honesty, in fact I'm quite confident America will continue to do the evil she has been demonically commissioned to do, yet I welcome America's challenge to prove me wrong with evident sincere contrite and redemptive change in her character.

6. Vietnam War Era

"I ain't got no quarrel with them Viet Cong . . . They never called me nigger."

Muhammad Ali

The Vietnam War was actually considered a Cold War Conflict since war was never really officially declared.

The conflict began November 1, 1955 and lasted till Saigon fell April 30, 1975.

Hippie peace movements and flower children as they were then called flourished all over the country protesting the Vietnam War and thousands upon thousands of draft dodgers were seeking exile and asylum in Canada, Mexico and other countries.

American solders were dieing in record numbers and African American solders were dieing in disproportionate record numbers with their names as well as the names of all American causalities spread across the television screen daily during the featured evening news.

African American families desperately glued their eyes to the Black and White television screen and waited with baited breath to see if the names of their loved ones drafted and sent of to fight a war that they couldn't even conceptualize or make sense of, but were assured that their sole purpose of military involvement was to protect Americans and an American interest that they didn't clearly understand, would appear on the news as "lost in combat". One of the interesting yet disturbing citizen information aspects of the Vietnam War was how few African Americans actually knew what the war was really all about. Muhammad Ali, like Malcolm X, contended that he had an oppressive enemy right here at home in America to fight and no need to travel across the globe to fight people who had done him no harm and posed him no threat.

Muhammad Ali (born Cassius Marcellus Clay Jr.; January 17, 1942) is a former American boxer and three-time World Heavyweight Champion, who is widely considered one of the greatest heavyweight championship boxers of all times.

Originally known as Cassius Clay, Ali changed his name after being inspired by preaching of Malcolm X, and joining the Nation of Islam in 1967; Ali refused to be conscripted into the Vietnam War. He was arrested and found guilty of draft evasion charges, stripped of his boxing title, and his boxing license was suspended. He was not imprisoned, but did not fight again for nearly four years while his appeal worked its way up to the U.S. Supreme Court, where it was successful. Another of the significant highlights for African Americans of the Vietnam War era would be the defunct Eartha Kitt.

Eartha Kitt, born in North Carolina, Eartha Mae Keith (January 17, 1927-December 25, 2008) she was an African American actress, singer and cabaret star. She was best known for her distinctive singing style, voice quality and her 1953 hit Christmas song "Santa Baby".

She took over the role of Catwoman with her signature "cat purr" sound for the third season of the 1960s Batman television series, replacing Julie Newmar who was unavailable for the final season.

In 1968 during the administration of President Lyndon Johnson, Mrs. Kitt encountered a substantial professional setback after she made anti-war statements during a White House luncheon.

Eartha Kitt was asked by Lady Bird Johnson what she thought of the Vietnam War.

She replied: "You send the best of this country off to be shot and maimed, no wonder the kid's rebel and take pot."

The remark reportedly caused Mrs. Johnson to burst into tears and led to the derailment of Ms. Kitt's career.

Publicly ostracized in the US, she devoted her energies to performances in Europe and Asia. She eventually returned to the United States able to get only very limited work and lived out the remainder of her life until she passed December 25, 2008.

African Americans have always pulsated to the rhythm of the time and reflected the circumstances of any given period in music and dance though this was the era of the Vietnam War and the usual added adversities Black's had to endure in America.

African American music though born of adversity was a reflection of the superlative royalty of African creative and masterful ancestors whom were naturally and rhythmically in sync with universal motion and the natural law and order of things all about the universe. In the redemption of the African American, Soul Music was an important effective assistant, though the threats and reminders of oppression were up front and center stage of the entertainment venues. African American musical artist like the late great Sam Cooke had already expressed to African Americans years earlier, that "A change is gonna come". Sam Cooke wrote "A change is gonna come", in dedication to Dr. Martin Luther King Jr. and the notorious Civil Rights March on Washington. The Temptations were singing "War what it is good for? Absolutely nothing", Edwin Star, sang; "Stop the War", Freda Payne, "Bring the boys home, bring them back alive", James Brown was singing "Say It Loud, I'm Black and I'm proud", Nina Simone "To Be Young Gifted and Black", Curtis Mayfield "Where Moving On Up, Lord Have Mercy We're Moving On UP".

In the midst of Civil Rights movement, Jim Crow, and multiple turmoil, African Americans were able through song, to hold on to their prophetic voices. African Americans danced in the streets of America as was commonly usual, exhibiting a cultural rhythmic inherent compassion and togetherness brought with them from mother Africa. All African Americans were in some way expressing enthusiasm and proudly advocating Black Power, liberation and awareness! And despite the Vietnam War that was going on, were restless, focused and united for one common goal, liberation.

The African American liberation flag (red, black and green, inherited from the great Marcus Garvey) flew all over the country and every Black organization and leadership imaginable was instrumental in raising the level of African American consciousness in all African American people weather the ideology of their branch of the African American movement was agreed with in part or totality.

As the era of civil rights is being enacted, Lo and behold! No rest for the weary, William B. Shockley, shocked! The African American community with his racist theory.

William B. Shockley is the Creator of Transistor and theory on Race. He preached a philosophy of "Retrogressive Evolution".

Stipulating that intelligence was genetically transmitted, he deemed Blacks genetically inferior to Whites and unable to achieve their intellectual level.

As a corollary, he suggested that Blacks were reproducing faster than whites-hence, the retrogression in the human evolution. Shockley's insult resonated long enough to serve as a reminder and confirmation of what we knew white America thought of African Americans.

African Americans remained conscious and skeptical of the savage and despicable un-human ways in which whites perceive them.

The events of the civil rights era which represented the un-binding of African Americans from second class citizenship, converted into "Affirmative Action" of which most American minorities benefited White women being the main benefactors.

African American women were encouraged to join the independent trend of the era which expressed independence from their Black men. Black woman were being encouraged to make it on their own without men, an ideal and suggestion that didn't require extra effort since African American woman were already in most instances the single parents and heads of households. This was just another systemic trick that years later proved fruitless and added to the demise of the African American family.

The remnants of this particular action have African American woman today shaking their heads when they hear how the rise of bi-racial relationships of which African American men are the most in demand regardless of criminal, educational and other thought to be deficient characteristics in their backgrounds.

Black women were perplexed with remembering that American society had preached to them with assiduous suggestion, demand

and insistence, that the Black man was no good and that the Black woman could do much better without him. This was certainly the same familiar strategy white Americans used to discourage African American interest in the "Mother Land" Africa during and prior to the civil rights era. The insisted that Africa was a primitive and savage land and African Americans were privileged to removed from such hideous and vile existence.

The socio economic events of Woman's Rights were quite rewarding economically to African American woman but the un-preparedness added to the devastations of the African American family, totally disconnecting a father from the household and raising children in "in-home isolation". The African American woman returns home from work and when her children come home from school they go right to their rooms and engage with computers and TV, while the mother retreats to her separate room, without any collective family communications. The mother has the "9-5 blues, ain't got a man blues, fatherless children blues".

Meals are rarely cooked in the home since most meals are gotten and consumed in school and generally outside the home eliminating more significant quality family time that could and should be spent collectively.

Essentially you have a family contained in a home of which no one communicates, ultimately making all household members strangers to each other.

When African American woman agreed to champion woman's right's and independence with their white counterparts, this was clearly not what they signed up for nor had in mind, they actually mistakenly thought their "right's and independence" experiences would reflect an entitlement of power similar to that of American white woman only to found out in the interim that they had been exploited, grossly misrepresented and misled.

Affirmative Action refers to policies that take factors including "race, color, religion, sex, or national origin" into consideration in order to benefit an underrepresented group, usually as a means to counter the effects of a history of discrimination.
In 1965 President Lyndon Johnson issued the Executive Order and in 1968 gender was added to the anti discrimination list. Affirmative Action was basically intended to facilitate the traditional American goals of assimilation and access to power. Affirmative Action provided an opportunity for African Americans and other minorities to get educations, degrees and jobs that would potentially lead them to participation in America's main stream social and economic arenas.

Towards the end of the civil rights era America was trying to repair her tarnished image in the world and was well on her way to super power status.
The Soviet Union's advancements in warfare technology added to frustrations and disenchantment of African American former slaves became America's main concerns. The African American Revolution was simmering down on many fronts but there was still active revolutionary movement in rare locations through out the country and Philadelphia, Pennsylvania was home to "MOVE" a revolutionary movement founded by John Africa and literally destroyed in 1985 after Philadelphia's first African American mayor, Wilson Goode ordered a C-4 bomb be dropped on a row of houses where MOVE

members lived killing eleven people including children and babies. The bomb burned 61 homes and left 250 people homeless.

The courts many years later ruled that excessive force had been used but no criminal charges were brought against the mayor that ordered the execution nor any other connected officials and authorities.

After the Vietnam War ended in 1975 and African American radical movements like the Black Panther Party begun to dissolve, the middle class African Americans adopted an "individualist" concept and disconnected themselves in every since of the word from the African American community. From the 1930s through the 1970s the middle class African Americans were an active and significant part of the Black community. Great prominent African American personalities like Langston Hughes, James Baldwin, Lorraine Hansberry and many others remained loyal and tightly connected to the Black community even when they lived abroad for any given period of time. The drastic disconnect of significant African American contributions in the form of leadership, economics, and other unlimited talents represented and posed a community culture shock and abandonment that would last for many painstaking years to come.

The evils of the new day and different order of things social, political and economic have surprised African Americans in their suburban communities thought to be secluded safe havens. The infectious discriminations of white American racism and hatred have now crossed over into the middle class African American suburban safe havens threatening their quality of life and overall existence.

7.   Rastafarian Movement

The movement of Jah! People

Rasta Mon Vibrations! Dread Locks! Jah! The Most High!

The Rastafarian movement became prevalent in the United States mainly during the early 1970s with what was visibly perceived to be a strange un-kempt cultural hair style known as Dread Locks.

The hair style or expression though at first seemed eccentric and primitive, slowly became acceptable, adoptable and very popular among African Americans with the Cultural Revolution and openness of the time.

The Rastafari movement proclaims itself to be a monotheistic, new religious movement that arose in a Christian culture in Jamaica West Indies in the 1930s. Its adherents, who worship Haile Salassie I of Ethiopia, former Emperor of Ethiopia (1930-1936 and 1941-1974), as God incarnate, the second advent, are known as Rastafarians, or Rastas.

The movement is sometimes referred to as "Rastafarianism", but this term is considered derogatory and offensive by some Rastas, who dislike being labeled as an "ism". Rastafari is a highly organized religion; it is a religion and an ideology.

Many Rastas say it is not a "religion" at all, but a "Way of Life". Most Rastas do not claim any sect or denomination, and thus encourage one another to find faith and inspiration within themselves, although some do identify strongly with one of the "mansions of Rastafari"-the three most prominent of these being the Nychbinghi, the Bobo Ashanti and the Twelve Tribes of Israel.

The name Rastafari is not taken from Ras Tafari, the pre-regnal title of Haile Salassie I, composed of Amharic Ras (literally "Head," an Ethiopian title equivalent to Duke), and Haile Salassie's pre-regnal given name, Tafari. Rastafari are generally distinguished for asserting the doctrine of Haile Salassie I, the former, and final, Emperor of Ethiopia, is another incarnation of the Christian God, called Jah.

They see Haile Salassie I, as Jah or Rastafari, who is the second coming of Jesus Christ onto the earth.

The Rastafari movement encompasses themes such as the spiritual use of cannabis and the rejection of western society (called Babylon, in reference more to the metaphoric Babylon of Christianity than to the historical Mesopotamian city state). It proclaims Africa (also "Zion") as the original birthplace of mankind, and embraces various Afro centric social and political aspirations such as the sociopolitical views and teachings of Jamaican publicist, organizer, and Black Nationalist Marcus Garvey (also often regarded as a prophet).

Today, awareness of the Rastafarian movement has spread throughout much of the world, largely through interest generated by Raggae music.

The most notable example being the Jamaican singer/songwriter Bob Marley who died in 1981. By 1997, there were around one million Rastafarian faithful worldwide. Rastafarian see Jah as being in the form of the Holy Trinity, that is God being the God the Father, God the Son, and the Holy Spirit. Rasta's say that Jah, in the form of the Holy Spirit (incarnate), lives within the human, and for this reason they often refer to themselves as "I". Furthermore, "I and I" is used instead of "We", and is used in this way to emphasize the equality between all people, in the recognition that the Holy Spirit within us all makes us essentially one and the same.

1975 was the year that the world and particularly people of African descent said farewell to the life and transition of His Royal Highness, Ethiopian Emperor Haile Salassie. The hair to a dynasty that traced its origins to the 13th century and from there by tradition back to King Solomon and the Queen of Sheba, Haile Salassie is a defining figure in both Ethiopian and African history.

8. Crack

The devil's white magic.

African American renaissance has always been periodic revival. They are usually historic pro-active movement periods of vigorous artistic, socio-cultural and intellectual activity and rebirth, "but not this time". Instead, the crack and aids epidemics caused a new type of renaissance to take place amongst African Americans that would be un-rewarding and filled with the utmost despair and destruction.

Crack cocaine the irrevocably definite destruction and exploitation of African America.

The ability to perceive and comprehend the magnitude of crack, and aids was by far more than African Americans could have possibly fathomed or imagined.

As the drug plague entered and consumed Black communities becoming common placed and crack cocaine strategically and inconspicuously poured abundantly into African American communities it became inevitable to connect guns to the equation for the protection of the drug product and monetary profit.

A regretfully significant number of African Americans were engulfed and consumed by the heroin drug epidemic during the late sixties but that proved almost minute compared to the crack cocaine devastations of the eighties, nineties and new millennium.

The African American community was struck with a traumatic attack by intelligence agencies of the Fascist regimes of the United States Government that poured the newest version of cocaine into Black communities, leaving the people of those communities either dead or numb and absolutely defenseless.

In the years of the heroin epidemic it was common to hear of "drug kings" being caught and their drug organizations seized, brought down and dismantled. This new pattern became extremely different and almost obsolete for the crack era, though it started out with the occasional arrest of major drug chiefs and cartels, the high profile arrests soon began to dissipate setting the focus on the local nickel and dime crack dealer who would become the African American community tyrant and adversary.

All eyes on him and ignore the big fish that authorize security clearances for the delivery of significant amounts of drugs into Black communities. Crack cocaine made its debut with the distinguishing desirable features of affordability to anyone seeking her pleasure enhancement, addiction and ultimate unsuspecting destruction.

Powder cocaine remained more costly and appealing to a select element of people many of whom would eventually graduate to crack cocaine for its effectiveness, convenience and affordability.

It eventually became abundantly clear that the focus of law enforcement was on cocaine however, that focus was specifically on crack cocaine and not powder cocaine which meant that white's overall that regularly used and sold cocaine would be overlooked, and intensified focus would be on African American crack users and dealers most of whom were in ghetto or impoverished Black neighborhoods. This newly implemented focus and practice by law enforcement meant that the upper echelon powder cocaine users were somewhat safe from the intense scrutiny of law enforcement and crack cocaine users and dealers were going to be perused, prosecuted, convicted and sentenced to the fullest extent of drug laws while powder cocaine users got a mere slap on the wrist when periodically encountered by law enforcement.

It's become rare even to this day for law enforcement agencies to make regular major drug bust leaving African American communities to wonder about the skills and effectiveness of law enforcement or the bigger picture of drug conspiracy in politics, government and law enforcement for the manipulating control of African American people and significant broad range national economic profit.

In America the moral issue of drugs is of very little concern to government as the main concern relating to drugs is really revenue and profit.

Many crack users spiraled so far out of control with their addictions that they became what would be known as M.I.C.A. (Mentally incompetent and chemically addicted) patients or people. Crack effectively destroyed many of African America's most gifted, talented and brilliant minds. This devastation was the true undoing of the African American family and community, placing children of drug affected parents and families into foster care and group homes if not united with other responsible family members to care for them. Sincere homage is due to African American grandparents especially grandmothers.

It is frightfully dreadful to dare imagine what might have become of the African American family at any point in African American history without the presence, wisdom, love, strength and conviction of our beloved African American grandmothers that tirelessly journeyed for countless years the entire gamut for the survival of their families. They have undoubtedly been the unsung heroes of African American history and must be duly recognized, saluted and honored for their sincere dedication and effective efforts to deliver their decedents even to this complex and conflicted point of human existence and progression as a race of oppressed yet determined people. African American grandparents insured throughout the centuries of African American existence that faith be maintained in the family despite the foreseeable drudgeries of futureless ness and hopelessness embedded in the African American odyssey.

Unfortunately the African American odyssey has brought African Americans of the 21st century to an unfamiliar junction where the African American homes and families have become transparently faithless and spiritually destitute. African American grandparents were already a nurturing and essential force to the development of family and community but now had the increased burden and responsibility of total care of grandchildren after losing their own children to the devastations of a death dealing device in the form of crack cocaine and its subordinates such as insanity, aids and murder.

Crack at first seemed like a magical demonic drug mainly due to the total consumption effect it had on individuals regardless of their desire to just try it once to experience its effectiveness. Crack became a drug so powerfully addictive that just one Crack user in a family was enough to cause entire stable family's to topple.

Crack has proven far beyond undisputable clear evidence, to be one of the most destructive elements to the African American community but something of a God send, to the United States Government and an evil racist White America, returning to them their full ability to control their former slaves by anesthetizing them.

It is a well known and clear fact that drugs especially crack have severely impeded African American progress adding to the disconnection of African American family, community and society overall.

Gene rationally many African Americans fear their own children due to societal created perpetual distance.

The African American family has been dysfunctional by sociological clinical definition since their arrival to the shores of America as chattel slave cargo in slave ships but never to the inconceivable mid air suspension state they've existed in for the past few decades. Just a few years prior to the introduction of Crack, the various levels of government removed the boundaries that once contained children. This new trend and law insured African American children would opportunistically be able to reach failure and demise at a much earlier and vulnerable age. Most of the components to the old schools or ways of discipline are credited for saving the lives, integrity, dignity and souls of the race while the removal of boundaries has resulted in generational social/cultural insecurity and rapid demise and destruction of African American people by way of the very youth that represent the future of the race. Is this coincidental or just another component to the vast equation of American racism? The answer is simplistically repeated several times and throughout every chapter of this book.

Our African American communities have spiraled completely out of control with the infestation of drugs, murder, aids, insanity and the uncontrollable use of guns.

Cultural morals and values began to dissipate immediately after the arrival and use of the devices of death, decay and destruction for African Americans.

Our young African American male children became the new merchants of this demonic drug and their parent's generation is for the most part their loyally addictive customers, a clear recipe for internal family and community deterioration and ultimate destruction. Territories ultimately became an issue as is usually the case in any business establishment; two bakeries side by side selling the exact same product can't co exist without territorial friction and pose a competition easy to result in conflict, and when illegal drugs are the product the conflict usually results in fatalities.

The other significant part to the equation of the Crack epidemic is the forgotten babies this demonic drug substance produced. The overlooked and ignored ramifications of the Crack epidemic in African American communities actually produced more than one generation of Crack Babies.

During the formative years of the Crack epidemic babies born unto Crack addicted mothers were taken from the mothers immediately after giving birth, treated for detoxification and then placed in agencies for adoption and foster care. The numbers to this travesty of babies being born Crack addicted and to Crack addicted mothers increased beyond all expectations and ultimately exceeded the budgets set in place for the maintenance of its remedial programs. This marked a change in hospital policy, allowing un-tested Crack addicted mothers to leave hospitals unscreened, and uncontested with their new born babies.

Unfortunately, within the past decades, death claimed multi-millions of the lives that fell victim to Crack's conquest and though Crack didn't claim the lives of all those in its path, the effectiveness of its power and persuasion lingers for generations.

There are presently two generations of Crack babies born since Crack's debut, and those two specific generations have matured into the young adults that stand before us today, many of whom are afflicted with severe attention deficit disorders, desperation for attention, zombie behavior, conflicted identity and biological chemistry imbalances inherited from drug addicted parents.

These are most of the young Black men that move about with their pants down and asses out, craving and begging for the type of attention normally afforded women without even realizing it, they act as if their asses are on fire and hotter than those of woman. Any man with confident identity would never ascribe to detestable and desperate attention craving behaviors that require him to render his ass to the world like a bitch (female dog) in heat. In a documentary aired repeatedly on cable TV about prison life, a fifty year old prisoner was interviewed and asked about tolerance of new prisoner arrivals wearing their pants sagging and he replied; "Ass ain't for woman, it's for men", he continued, "I tell new young arrivals that they can give the ass up the easy way or the hard way, and I prefer the hard way".

The mere lack of identity amongst children born of the Crack epidemic/

Culture makes it easy for them to disregard, disrespect and devalue the identities of others and the histories connected to those identities. The Crack culture has in many ways influenced the youth born unto it, impeding their rationale and caused their human moral and value systems to become severely compromised.

The flip side of the coin presents young Black women who in their ignorance and desperation for a man have begun the tradition of settling for whatever is readily available to them. They like their male counterparts, feel undeserving of better quality in companionship since they were never guided in the direction of better things in life nor presented with ideal role model examples.

Certainly; herein, lays the classic example of two wounded solders headed towards fighting in battles and conflicts that they already know are hopeless for them and can't win.

Perhaps we subconsciously deny the long term effects of Crack on our children that are born of it, nonetheless the effects are real and may we be reminded that our present conditions are connected to our past and that that's in store for our future is also determined by our past.

Various or different types of influences shape our intellect and Crack has influenced and affected the order of things in the world today.

9.   AIDS

Extermination Of The Black Race

African Americans are either on the way to higher racial existence or racial extermination; hence African Americans are confronted with the death struggle of the different races of the world in a scramble for the survival of the fittest race.

When God created the world, and all therein, He handed a human authority over to the human beings He created and in time some would abuse that authority with the taints of an envy desiring oppressive and evil behavior. Behind the scene furthering scientifically advanced attempts to exterminate the African and African American.

AIDS is a fair indication of what will happen to the weaker people of the world in the near future when the stronger races will have developed themselves to the position of complete mastery of all things material. They will not then as they have not in the past, allow a weak and defenseless race to stand in their way, especially if in their doing so they will endanger their happiness, their comfort and their pleasures.

The AIDS pandemic as worldwide spread as it is with major concentration among people of color, particularly Black people, are not collectively having the discussions and conversations about it as they should.

More than a decade ago when AIDS appeared before the African American community and the world, it was initially perceived and suggested to be a disease exclusive to the Gay and Haitian communities. This type of stigma reserved for the Gay and Haitian communities made it a relatively easy topic to be discussed by the African American community and those outside the Black community.

Not only was there room for discussion on the topic of AIDS and the first infected communities, but the un-informed speculative discussions provided room within them for ridicule and mockery of the first AIDS victims. Nonetheless, in just a matter of a couple of years the fatalities resulting from the devastations of AIDS had escalated far beyond anything ever witnessed or imagined in American and world history and what began as a epidemic soon blossomed into a pandemic.

The discussion amongst African Americans about HIV/AIDS went from an easy topic for discussion so long as it didn't cross the fictitiously safe secure African American divide.

Regretfully the conspired and strategically rumored inaccurate information that had been sold to the African American community caused them to retreat to a "gagged" seclusion on the subject of HIV/AIDS once the virus crossed over into the heterosexual community and infected it more severely than the initial Gay and Haitian communities.

The greatest dilemma to the HIV/AIDS crisis in the African American community is clearly the silence.

The silence about the disease might be more fatal than the disease itself partly because the silence prevents probable/possible infected persons from testing, screening, treatment, and un-accountable for the further spread of the virus. The silence by the African American community on the devastatingly urgent issue of HIV/AIDS is what allows young African American men to return to the African American community from periods of incarceration, and during which time significant numbers of them became infected with the HIV/AIDS virus, and unsuspectingly silently infecting African American women.

According to national statistics, more than 95% of the inmate populations of state and federal prison institutions are HIV/AIDS infected. The HIV/AIDS crisis is realistically so far out of control in the African American community that the stigma and intense silence produced by it should be reversed to the ultimate level of intensified pro-active noise, discussion and collective community crisis intervention.

For several unfortunate frightful and psycho/socio reasons African Americans won't have the much needed community discussions and conversations about the reality of HIV/AIDS and how best to implement local community intervention and awareness programs.

Even Black leadership and clergy won't bring the issue of HIV/AIDS before the people and instead, leave the matter to the discretion of a hate driven, racist, questionable government to deal with and do as it deems fit.

The hate and racism that African Americans experience is multi dimensional and multi faceted running even the un-imaginable gamut of conspiracies from slavery to extermination.

AIDS (Acquired Immune Deficiency Syndrome) is a disease of the human immune system caused by the Human Immunodeficiency Virus (HIV). This condition progressively reduces the effectiveness of the immune system and leaves individuals susceptible to opportunistic infections and tumors. HIV is transmitted through direct contact of a mucous membrane or the bloodstream with a bodily fluid containing HIV, such as blood, semen, vaginal fluid, preseminal fluid, and breast milk. This transmission can involve anal, vaginal or oral sex, blood transfusion, contaminated hypodermic needles, exchange between mother and baby during pregnancy, childbirth, breastfeeding or other exposure to one of the previous noted bodily fluids.

Dr. Robert Strecker of Los Angles, California, a practicing gastroenterologist with a Ph.D. in pharmacology, was hired as a consultant to work on a health care proposal for an HMO of the Security Pacific Bank, concerning coverage costs in the event any of 30,000 employees came down with AIDS.

Along with the help of his brother, Theodore, a lawyer, the two compiled extensive research of the epidemic which ultimately became the Strecker Memorandum. In it, Dr. Strecker indicated that the AIDS virus in fact developed by the National Cancer Institute, in cooperation with World Health Organization (WHO), in a laboratory facility at Ft. Dietrick in Maryland.

From 1970-74, this laboratory facility was part of the U.S. Army's germ warfare unit, known as the Army Infectious Disease Unit, or Special Operations Division, also referred to as the Army's Chemical Biological Warfare Laboratory. Post 1974, the facility was renamed the National Cancer Institute (NCI). According to research William

Cooper (former Navy Intelligence), noted in Larry Jamison's article is The AIDS Virus Man Made? This work was supervised by the CIA under a project called MK-NAOMI.

Dr. Strecker traced some of the research and researchers at Ft. Dietrick/NCI to a group of Japanese scientists captured at World War two's end and given amnesty in exchange for information on racial and ethnic bio-weaponry, their research dated back to 1930. What's more, expatriated Russian scientists were brought in to help as well.

Dr. Strecker, one of the original and foremost authorities on the AIDS virus, found that the virus creation was conducted under the leadership of Dr. Robert Gallo, who later claimed to discover the virus.

Dr. Gallo and his team created the AIDS virus by combining the bovine (cattle) Leukemia virus and VISNA (sheep) virus, and injecting them into human tissue cultures. They discovered, as Dr. Strecker did, the bovine leukemia virus is lethal to cattle, but not to humans. And the VISNA virus is deadly to sheep, but not to man. However, when combined, they produce a retro-virus that can change the genetic composition of the cells they enter.

We must not forget the previous **Tuskegee Syphilis Experiment** (also known as the Tuskegee Syphilis Study or Public Health Service Syphilis Study) which was a clinical study conducted between 1932 and 1972 in Tuskegee, Alabama, by the U.S. Public Health Service.

Investigators recruited 399 impoverished African American sharecroppers with syphilis for research related to the natural progression of the untreated disease.

The Public Health Service, working with the Tuskegee Institute, began the study in 1932. Nearly 400 poor African American men with syphilis from Macon County, Alabama, were enrolled in the study.

For their participation in the study, the men were given free medical examinations, free meals and free burial insurance. They were never told that they had syphilis, nor were they ever treated for it.

According to the Center for Disease Control, the men were told they were being treated for "bad blood", a local term used to describe several illnesses, including syphilis, anemia and fatigue.

These are just some of the hatefully sadistic and evil conspiracies of historically racist governments like America with strong imperialistic ambitions and should strike thoughtful African Americans as being threatening and extremely dangerous.

It is for certain, only through appreciation of self will African Americans be able to rise to that higher quality of life that will enable them to avoid becoming an extinct race in the future, and instead become a race of people fit in every essential aspect and prepared and determined to survive and sustain themselves.

African Americans must revisit the "self worth" part of their spirits and souls for inspiration and rejuvenation, and then reclaim its essence despite the demonic attempts by racist hateful systems created in American government, to marginalize and exterminate the race.

The lack of responsible attention that we African Americans give to most urgent matters is also unfortunately demonstrated in our lack of attention given to the fatal omen of death among African Americans called AIDS.

10.   Bring in the Guns!

Heaven help the child that won't reach twenty one
Heaven help the man that gave that boy a gun
Lord hear our call when we fall, heaven help us all
Stevie Wonder

Wars and guns during America's formative years were a prelude to the culture of violence and race hatred that would inevitably engulf the entire country and take its place of permanency in America's infrastructure.

The African American underclass exhibit indelible traces of their severe oppression in modern Americanism and their dispensability in post modern Americanism; relative to political powerlessness and socio-economic depression, and subversive subcultures now dominated by drugs, guns, disease and murder which are clear evident forms of terrorism in African American communities. In the very same way that American government uses its law enforcement intelligence resources to monitor and control the local politics and economics of the African American community, they utilize those same resources to manipulatively insert drugs and guns into the African American communities for control, and overall economic profit.

Guns introduced a simplistic way for drug dealers to protect themselves as well as their product, profit and turf. The gun made the smallest, fearful and most timid man a force to reckon with, the gun gave him the power of persuasion and neutralization. Guns poured into the African American communities almost as rapid as crack did and young African American men had no qualms or reservations about either possession or use of them. A new feeling of instant power overwhelmed young African American men, leaving them with no alternatives to channel their newly discovered energies so their shootings similar to those of Police brutes became indiscriminate, contagious and a new prevailing major destructive element in the African American community.

WHEN MAN LOSES HIS VIRTUES HE BECOMES DESTRUCTIVE WITHOUT STRENGTH AND ONLY RESPECTS FORCE WHICH HE CANNOT COUNTERACT.

Intended targets were often missed and unintended innocent by passers and very young children were almost routinely mistakenly shot and often times killed.

This new trend of gun violence was most prevalent in African American communities every where in the country raising statistical murder rates far exceeding record breaking levels. Our young African American men became intrigued with the velocity of guns and quite obsessed with the guns ability to settle scores of most magnitudes especially drug related debts, turf squabbles and personal offenses. Some where in the mid eighties drugs and guns began to convert the behavior and image of African American young men into societal villains.

One of the most profoundly prevalent issues among young African Americans regarding their seniors is that they don't value or respect very much of what their elders claim to be convicted to, since they reluctantly realize their senior generation disconnected from them and became incapable of protecting their own families and communities, especially during their formative and very youthful years. This seemed to be an unfortunate, significant era for African Americans where their losses superseded their gains.

Civil Rights and Affirmative Action allowed African Americans into the mainstream of American socio-economics but the trade off would be the loss of the already circumstantially emotionally frail African American women, children and ultimately the family. This was the classic African American sell out, where African Americans for a very small price of what seemed to be a glamorous liberty and the pursuit of happiness walked away from their children, forgetting to take them along with them though they got nothing but tricked in the interim anyway which bought on the disrespect and callous inconsideration by their children.

African American youth of the 21st century see their elder generation as being the worst compromising people imaginable and far worse than their previous courageous ancestors.

It is for certain no coincidence that a disproportionate number of African American men are incarcerated as a direct result of government conspired and perpetual drug and gun culture.

Laws changed quickly allowing disadvantaged and misdirected fifteen year olds to be prosecuted as adult's for specific newly prevalent felony crimes, such as drugs, guns and murders, extracting from the African American community and herding our young Black male children to prisons at an earlier age and disproportionately alarming rate for the purpose of isolation and emasculation.

Most of them neither old enough nor mature enough to know and clearly understand the government has conspired intent to set a stage that is deliberately designed by the evils of a racist white American power machine for the ultimate demise of young Black men and the toppling domino effect on the African American community. In most cases these African American youth are given the worst minimal legal counsel and usually before being assigned legal counsel, incriminated themselves when interrogated, not realizing as under age youth, that the police ask questions for the purpose of convicting you, by no means are they ever attempting to defend your "presumption of innocence until proven guilty". The disparities of the African American family and community made it very easy for young Black males to walk right into the open awaiting hands of expert oppressors who strategically designed and implemented systems that would present their maze of despair and self destruction.

Racism is one of the easiest institutions to implement amongst destitute peoples. Destitution and poverty is what made Africans so vulnerable, and ethnic genocide so simplistic in places like; Rwanda, Darfur, Uganda and many other conflicted locations in the African continent.

When men are hungry they will vulnerably resort to whatever is required of them to achieve a piece of bread.

The same manipulation by the Belgians of the Africans in Rwanda encouraging and inciting the murders of more than eight million Africans is identical to the evil manipulation in America driven by a hatefully racist white government that encourages and enables the murders of millions of African Americans through instruments of destruction such as guns, drugs, disease and overall poverty.

There might be some accuracy to the assumption that the eradication of guns and drugs in the African American community would resolve the issue of disproportionate murder.

One of the main components to any discussion about guns and drugs that continuously goes unmentioned or minutely focused on, is where these guns and drugs come from, and only after serious acknowledgement of the root source of distribution in African American communities of these threatening vises will African Americans be able to move forward to the prevention of entry and access into Black communities of death devices such as guns and drugs. African Americans keep forgetting that guns and drugs are neither manufactured, nor ware-housed in the African American community, the African American community merely provides a despairing market place for these and significant other detrimentally threatening toxic desires so they're invited welcomed and poured in abundantly and the drift towards disaster continues. Every so often the question arises, where are these guns coming from and how are they getting into the hands of our children?

And the answer is simplistic!

The same enemy that is arming the world is also arming our children. The might of America was acquired with the gun which has grown rapidly each year sense its invention and is unfortunately but realistically likely to continue to grow in popularity and demand.

Therefore, it behooves the African American community to create intensive "Gun Education" programs so that at the very least our youth can be taught the serious danger, power, purpose and proper use of guns. Like most whites, Blacks should become responsible legal owners of guns with an educated understanding and serious consideration of its potential dangers.

African Americans in their challenge against the racist and bigoted driven evils of white America are often told by white Americans that they (white's) don't share the same racist desires and practices as their parents and believe in equality and everyone's right to co-exist regardless of their race, religion and any other social or cultural differences. This position by whites has been expressed for numerous years, especially since the civil rights era of the late 1960s, and has proven fruitless leaving African Americans asking the repetitive question? Why do white Americans continue to have vehement hatred for African Americans and an urgent thirst to kill them even in the 21st century?

Decades ago whites used the then popular excuse, that African American youth were playing with toy guns that appeared real, the toy guns were immediately removed from children's hands in hopes that it would save their lives from routine racist police killings, non-the less the killing sprees continued with the new excuse for executing African American youth which became "we thought they had a gun, or the wallet and cell phone looked like it might have been a gun".

The clear point here is that whites will never stop their hate and killing black men on a morality basis, they're incapable of such civilized peaceful, co-existence, compassionate behavior and practices due to their evil genetic DNA make up. Those that don't kill local African Americans and other minorities through American law enforcement agencies have no qualms with the millions of atrocious murders of overseas foreign people of color for the mere purpose of American economic special interest.

Caucasians are the most impervious and coldest race of people ever known to mankind.

11.   Million Man March

The journey of a thousand miles starts with the first step.

Immersed in a drug and AIDS epidemic, out of control murder and crime rate, all of these plagues had become common household words in the African American community and the mention and commonality of either no longer caused African Americans to cringe. Murder, drugs and crime were discussed with a new and unusual air of normalcy in Black communities across America.

The United States government had just coined the new phrase "Racial tolerance" and enacted it supposedly in hopes to reduce prevalently severe levels of racism.

The O. J. Simpson murder trial had just ended October 3, 1995 with O.J. Simpson's verdict delivered by jurist who found O.J. Simpson "not guilty". This was the most publicized case in American history lasting nine months. By the end of the O. J. Simpson criminal trial, national surveys showed dramatic differences between most blacks and most whites in terms of their assessment of O. J. Simpson's guilt. Most African Americans believed Simpson to be guilty but welcomed with anticipation and jubilation his acquittal for the centuries of injustices done continuously to Blacks who never got equally due legal consideration and fair trails.

This victory of justice for Simpson and black America turned the whitest of faces red and intensified white America's hatred and racism. African Americans have always had to celebrate tiny victories as though they were big ones and the O.J. Simpson victory was one of those small victories that felt big because of the un-due and unlimited injustices the American justice system has always disfavor ably represented to African Americans.

1995 was un-doubt ably a year of decadence and regretfully similar to the years before and after it.

While African Americans throughout the country were loathing in demoralizing agony a man among them was divinely inspired with an avant-garde approach and an action plan to repair damage and reignite campaigns for community development and an economic tier.

Minister Louis Farrakhan of the Nation of Islam initially the predecessor of Malcolm X upon Malcolm's expulsion from the Nation of Islam under the leadership of Elijah Muhammad and the only remaining African American leader cut from the wise and authentic dedicated cloth of genuine African American leadership, conceived a brilliant idea of African American mobilization by way of a march on the nations capital and decided it should be a Million Man March.

MAN IS THE INDIVIDUAL WHO IS ABLE TO SHAPE HIS OWN CHARACTER, MASTER HIS OWN WILL, DIRECT HIS OWN LIFE AND SHAPE HIS OWN ENDS.

Minister Louis Farrakhan was for certain the one leader of African American people that escaped the many attempts the white racist media and government conspirators made to assassinate his character and physical life like most of his predecessors. Despite those failed attempts Minister Farrakhan emerged stronger, wiser and evidently more strategic in his struggle for the liberation and empowerment of African American people and despite his arduous endeavors always managed to be the last man standing. Because of his ingenious God given ability to weather the disparities of time, Minister Louis Farrakhan's thinking was well re-invented and produced a magnificent divine concept. He didn't need a come back song or story since he had never left the struggle and plight of his people, his continuous dedicated work and aspiration was the up-lifting of his people whom he never abandoned.

Here was a man whose melodic voice and majestic presence commanded the undivided attention of Black people everywhere he was seen or heard as he firmly and charismatically maintained his magical ability of tenacious articulate clarity and inspirational persuasion and was still determined to achieve African American triumphalism.

African American history is made on October 16, 1995 in Washington. DC with the journey from all across America of more than a million Black men to the Washington National Mall for the Million Man March conceived and organized by Minister Louis Farrakhan.

Minister Louis Farrakhan quite disturbed at seeing African America on the brink of disaster and destruction felt an urgent need to call all African American men together in a unity mass meeting on the Washington Mall to discuss and remedy the fast paced deterioration and destruction of African American communities throughout the nation and suggested the day be also utilized as a day for African American Atonement.

The melodically eloquent Minister Louis Farrakhan, delivered a brilliant speech which entailed a verbal pledge by all African American men in attendance, and the ministers plan additionally included all the other necessary components of an effective pro active plan to be executed by Black men in their African American communities immediately on their return home from the Million Man March.

THE FUNCTION OF THE PRESS OR MEDIA IS PUBLIC SERVICE WITHOUT PREJUDICE OR PARTIALITY, TO CONVEY THE TRUTH AS IT IS SEEN AND UNDERSTOOD WITHOUT FAVORITISM OR BIAS.

The Million Man March was an overwhelming success that re-defined the African American plight, though, the racist American White media, disturbed by the mere attempt of Black men uniting for the purpose of urgently needed African American community remedial action, attacked the march with its racist and skillful chicanery.

The white racist American media wanted national and world viewers to think that only an insignificant few people attended the march and emphatically down played the numbers of those actually in attendance. Camera's and all other technical methods of actual counts by government agencies and March counters revealed true historic record breaking numbers. The media's attack was expected and calculated into the initial planning but had almost no impact or effect on the goals of millions of Black men who were filled with jubilation and inspiration similar to that of incidents of miraculous proportion descriptively written about only in religious scriptures. This historic march filled the atmosphere of America with a welcomed and much needed hope that transformed into the production of critically needed programs and resources for Black communities by African Americans of every religious, political and social persuasion imaginable.

Black men put aside their many ideological differences and stood on the common principals of "unity" and "action" and clearly understood and agreed that action is the greatest antidote of despair.

The focus was solely on essential and urgent issues that concerned the fate of every Black man, woman and child in America. African American radio and media, Christian clergymen and organizations were at the forefront working in a spirited rhythmic lock-step motion, side by side with Minister Farrakhan, the Nation of Islam and every Black group and organization involved in the Million Man March.

The African American churches and clergy throughout America were critically essential in the inception and planning phases of the march.

African American churches across the country allowed their houses of worship to be used as bases for organizing the March and command centers for controlling the march.

The authenticity and concentrated focus of this mass mobilization welcomed supporters but didn't require cheerleaders.

More than a decade after the Million Man March, African Americans are asking the question; "what happened", and the answer is simply that the African American community must continuously periodically be re-energized and the responsibility of that re-fortification doesn't belong to just one man and one idea. Young African Americans must now without further hesitation step up to their inherited role of un-compromised responsibility and leadership for the African American family and community. African Americans must immediately become the very leaders that they're looking for. African Americans must collectively become financially literate then develop autonomous communities with a financial base capable of initiating and providing for the community's survival, sustainability, creativity and resources.

I believe in one God (Allah), and I believe that God (Allah) had one religion…that He inspired all His Prophets with Moses, Jesus, Muhammad, and all the others…they all had one doctrine and that doctrine was to give clarification of humanity and glorification to the oneness of Allah (God).

Allah Hu Akbar!
(Allah is Greatest)

12.   Conversion to Islam

The Holy Prophet Muhammad, Had Before Him A Very Grand Object-The Reformation First Of The Arabs And Then Of The Whole World.

The business of incarceration of young African American men began to boom stimulating the economy and requiring the need for more jails to be built to house particularly young Black male prisoners.

It has been common practice since the days of ancient civilizations "and notably that of the story of Jesus as a baby possessing potential divine ambitions but was being sought to be killed by Herod," that the most historically powerful nations of any given period in time, commonly target the young males for extermination heading off that nations ability to advance.

About 10.4% of the entire African American male population in the United States aged 25 to 29 was incarcerated by the end of 2002, according to a Justice Department report released in July 2003 and by far the largest racial or ethnic group-by comparison, 2.4% of Hispanic men and 1.2% of White men in the same age group were incarcerated. According to a report by the Justice Policy Institute in 2002, the number of Black men in prison has grown to five times the rate it was twenty years ago. Today, more African American men are in jail than in college. In 2000 there were 791,600 Black men in prison and 6030,032 enrolled in college. In 1980 there were 143,000 Black men in prison and 463,700 enrolled in college. These African American incarceration statistics reflect numbers reported in July 2003 but have since increased at an alarming much higher rate.

The justice system provided promising careers with the repetitious open and replenishing long term open season on Black men, particularly the youth.

A significant feature of the present century is the new and wide-spread trend of Islamic revival. After a long period of stagnation the world of Islam is rising from its stupor. A new awakening has appeared on the horizon, a new life is being infused into the world communities of Islam. This trend is visible in every country and at every place and has within it the possibilities of its becoming the harbinger of a new age.

But this revivalist trend can become the messenger of a New Age only if it is accompanied by an intellectual revolution-a thorough appraisal of the intellectual and cultural heritage of Islam and its representation to the world in the language of today.

A major concern that had been overlooked blossomed into a magnitude unimaginable to government and American society. Since the American pursuit of happiness pertained to the minuscule few Blacks and mostly whites, young Black men canceled the centuries of false hopes and promises of American democracy and moved forward after everything else contained in the American dream failed them, to a religion that was inherently familiar to their souls having already been the original religion of African people in the land where they originally derived from.

The religion spoken of here is the same religion that white enslavers made a concentrated forceful effort to rid the African American slave of, and clearly a main component needing eradication for successfully permanently breaking the spirit of slaves.

TAKE AWAY THE HIGHEST IDEAL FOR MAN-FAITH AND CONFIDENCE IN A GOD-AND MANKIND AT LARGE IS REDUCED TO SAVAGERY.

Similar to the pagan Arabs before the advent of the Prophet Muhammad (PBUH), but on a significantly much smaller and perhaps domicile scale, African Americans were immensely engrossed in degenerate behavior while worshiping America's only legal God, which is the God of Christianity. Until a few decades ago any religion other than Christianity in America was considered and treated as a form of taboo communism which was quite clearly the case for the repulsed arrival of the religion of Islam in America.

America historically and pretentiously represents the epitome of freedom and is considered the ultimate symbol of freedom throughout the free world yet, ironically has millions of African American citizens that have left her so called "free Christian American ideals" and flocked in record breaking numbers embracing a religion known as "Islam" the religion of humanity and spitefully with resentment considered by evil racist white America to be an oppressive religion.

However! While African Americans were rotting under severe oppression and disparity, Islam arrived in America to deal a death blow to oppression, injustice, and call all who would heed, to the oneness of Allah (God). African American Christians, like many foreign Muslims are incidentally Christian, clearly meaning; that whatever country they might have been born in they would have ascribed to the religion of that land.

This is quite different for African American Muslim decedents of slaves who have embraced the religion of Islam solely by choice despite historically racist oppression and anti-Islamic sentiment and resistance from white America.

The direct route to Allah, the Beneficent, the Merciful and the fastest growing religion in America and the world with its perfect guidance and divine legislation for Muslim adherents in the form of the Holy Qur'an, Allah's revelation to his holy prophet Muhammad, the Muslims and to all of humanity.

Monotheism; Taw heed (The belief in one God, Allah) and the delightful thought of an adjoining theocratic government appealed to young African American men and women desiring a direct channel to the Supreme Being and creator. In this uncompromising monotheism, with its simplistic, enthusiastic faith in the supreme rule of a transcendent being lays the chief strength of Islam. Its adherents enjoy a consciousness of contentment and resignation unknown among followers of most if not all creeds.

Allah, according to the most correct of the opinions respecting it, is the proper name applied to the Being who exists necessarily by Himself, comprising all the attributes of absolute perfection.

The religion of humanity, that turned imbedded uncertainties in the minds of young African Americans into Devine confidence and causing them to immediately discharge their Muslim duties of submission, devotion, patience and obedience to Allah. Muslims are taught and encouraged to have unshakable belief in the existence of Allah (God), for unless a man has firm and unshakable faith in Allah's (God) existence, how can he render obedience to him? Faith, thus, is firm belief arising out of knowledge and conviction.

The individual who knows and reposes unshakable belief in the unity of Allah (God), in His Attributes, in His Law and the Revealed Guidance, and in the Divine Code of Reward and Punishment is called Mo'min (faithful).

This faith invariably leads an individual to a life of obedience and submission to the will of Allah (God) and one who lives this life of submission is known as a Muslim.

Muslims ascribe to the essential fundamentals known as the Five Pillars of Islam which are acts of devotion, and commit their lives to the important practice of each.

(1) The first Pillar is known as "Iman" (faith), which begins for new converts to the religion of Islam, with the declaration of faith known as "Shahada". Iman, means faith and is a term designating the articles of belief that are a part of Islam. Iman is defined as faith in Allah (God), His Angels, His books (revelations), His Prophets, and the Day of Judgment.

(2) The second Pillar is Salat or Salah the canonical or ritual prayer, as opposed to the spontaneous petitioning of Allah (God) which is called "dua". Salat consist of a series of movements and recitations, and is thus a ritual, more of liturgy, or an act of worship, than the supplication usually associated with the word "prayer" in the West.

As an act of worship, the Salat is a yoga which models the body, mind, and soul-the latter in the form of speech-to the invisible prototype of awakened consciousness, or of the individual aware of Allah (God). The performance of Salat (prayer) five times daily is obligatory, beginning at the age of reason, which is deemed to be seven years old. The obligatory Salat (prayer) is however, one of the Five Pillars of Islam and is clearly the most important after the Shahadah (declaration of faith).

(3) The third Pillar is Zakat or Zakah (akin to mean "purification" from the verb Zaka which signifies "to thrive", "to be wholesome", and "to be pure"). The giving up of a portion of the wealth one may possess, in excess of what is needed for substance, to "purify" or legitimize what one retains. Zakat is one of the Five Pillars of Islam and is in effect a tax on one's possessions.

It may be used for the upkeep of the poor, for those who own less than that prescribed for the paying of Zakat and who have no earning capacity; for the destitute; Muslims in debt through pressing circumstances; travelers in need; those serving the cause of Islam, and fighting in the way of Allah (God); for slaves to buy themselves out of bondage; for benevolent works. Those who collect tax on behalf of the state for disbursement are also allowed to take the needs of their livelihood from it.

(4) The fourth Pillar is Sawn (Fasting) The Prophet Muhammad (P.B.U.H.) recommended fasting as a spiritual discipline. It was taken up by the early Muslims so enthusiastically that finally the Prophet had to curtail it because excessive fasting by the Companions in Medina was making them physically weak. **Ramadhan** is the ninth month of the Arab and Islamic calendar. The word Ramadhan originally meant "great heat", a description which originates in the

pre-Islamic solar calendar. This month was holy in Arab tradition before the Prophet Muhammad's (PBUH) reform of Islam and was one of the months of truce. Fasting during the holy month of Ramadhan is one of the Five Pillars of Islam. The fasting month of Ramadhan begins with the physical sighting of the new moon. If the new moon is not sighted on the twenty-eighth day of the previous month, this may be lengthened to twenty-nine or thirty days so that the beginning of the fasting may correspond with the beginning of the month of Ramadhan. During Ramadhan a Muslim does not eat or drink from daybreak, when a thread of light may be seen on the horizon, until the sun has set. Before the sunset prayer (maghrib), the fast is broken with three dates and water, then after the prayer a breakfast is eaten.

Somewhat later in the night a larger meal is taken. It is common to take a meal, sometimes called Suhur, in the early morning before the fast begins.

Musicians and criers of Muslim communities threw out the world walk through towns at night to wake the people to take this meal; the criers often do this as a pious act.

(5) Hajj (pilgrimage), also one of the Five Pillars of Islam, is an elaborate series of rites, requiring several days for their accomplishment, performed at the Grand Mosque of the holy city of Mecca and in the immediate environs of the city, at a particular moment of the Islamic year, which because of the lunar calendar, advances some ten days each year. The Hajj (pilgrimage) is obligatory upon those who can "make their way" to the Holy city of Mecca. That is to say that the requirement is not absolute, but incumbent upon those whose health and means permit it, and who, in doing so, do not compromise their responsibilities towards their

families. Those who have made the Hajj (pilgrimage) are entitled to prefix their names with the appellation "Pilgrim" (Al-Hajj). From every part of the world Muslims journey to Mecca to perform the Hajj (pilgrimage) during the designated Hajj season and the number of pilgrims can easily reach into the millions. After the degenerate behavior of the pagan Arabs, the Prophet Muhammad (PBUH) gave a new model based upon his two pilgrimages after the reforming of Islam; the pilgrimage of the year 7 of the Hijrah (March 629), after the treaty of Hudaybiyyah, and the "farewell" pilgrimage of the year 10 (March 632). The latter was the more important from the point of view of exemplary situations. However, the holy Qur'an says that the founder of the rite of pilgrimage to the sacred house is the Prophet Abraham (Ibrahim) PBUH.

African American young incarcerated men particularly were embracing the religion of Islam by numbers only seen during the historical Jihad's and Crusade's.

A "War" in Islam is a Jihad. A Jihad is a noble sacred fight in the way of Allah for the verification of a Muslim society that seeks to free man from cruelty, oppression and aggression.

Young African American men used their newly found religion of Islam to cleanse their souls, liberate their minds and educate themselves in ways unlikely beyond the prison gates or social confinement of severely impoverished and disenfranchised African American communities. Most new African American young converts to Islam had never in their lives prayed or believed in any God and basically had no religious connections as the environments that they subjectively dwelled in conditioned them and dictated to them that they live solely in the here and now moment for survival and instant physical satisfaction and gratification. These young men and women converts observed immediately that Islam was a natural humanitarian liberating religion with strong emphases on true justice, righteous behavior and human equality which are attractive virtues to all righteous human beings. This religion of Islam, contradicted misogyny of woman and taught with encouraging principles, the equality and rights of all women.

The first person to believe in the divinely prophetic mission of the Holy Prophet Muhammad (P.B.U.H.) was a woman by the name of; Khadejah who eventually became His wife. Young Black men learned to love, respect and protect their women and all woman.

UNLESS MAN INCREASES IN WISDOM AS MUCH AS
IN KNOWLEDGE, INCREASE IN KNOWLEDGE WILL
BE AN INCREASE IN SORROW.

America being the presumptive Christian society she is, never in her wildest dream conceived that the descendents of former African American slaves would return to the oneness of their own original true God, Allah and religion of Islam.

One of America's main concerns with the rapid growth of Islam in America and particularly among young African Americans is the potential of their becoming politically active. Caucasian Euro-American Jews intensely share this same concern since Muslims now out-number Jews in American population.

It should be known before further venture into discussion that the original Jews are African, from such tribes as; the tribe of Falasha. Falasha, are a native Hebrew/Jewish tribe of Ethiopia whose origin goes back before the 2D, century B.C. They trace their ancestry to King Solomon and the Queen of Sheba. Prior to the birth of Moses and during his lifetime, which became known as the Mosaic period, Black Egyptians enslaved Black Israelites.

Moses no doubt was of the Black race as were the Egyptians.

He spent forty years in Pharaoh's palace among the Black Egyptians, passing as Pharaoh's grandson. It's apparent that in order for him to have "passed" as the Pharaoh's grandson, he had to have looked just like the Egyptians among whom he lived.

The popular issue of anti-Semitism has resorted to the myth of a Jewish race in an attempt to justify itself and to provide a pseudo-scientific cloak for its political and economic motives through out the world. Caucasian European Jews converted to Judaism at different periods in history and are not from the original tribes of Isreal. The findings of physical anthropologists and Biblical explanations cited in an array of available research books clearly conclude that Caucasian Jews are not a separate racial group.

This statement is true for both Black and White groups who practice Judaism. Even if a Jewish race existed today, the descendants of the Hebrew-Isrealites of antiquity would be the group of people to which a Jewish race refers and not European Caucasian Jews.

Many people are erroneously inclined to believe that the word "Jew" refers only to Caucasian people who practice Judaism. This is incorrect and a total fallacy. The word "Jew" came into usage after the words "Hebrew" and "Isrealite". Its original meaning refers to the people who came from Judea, which at that time was only part of the larger Isrealite nation.

Caucasian Euro-American Jews rose to preeminence in the United States after World War II and developed what became a traditional alliance with African Americans against caste discrimination in the United States.

European Caucasian Jews broke with the Civil Rights alliance in the late 1960s when the goals of African Americans in the Civil Rights movement shifted from demands for political and legal equality to demands for economic equality.

Euro-American Caucasian Jews then relentlessly and insensitively moved front and center stage to join in on the profitable exploitation of African Americans. Their inherent coldness and clannishness enables them to switch gears at any point of action and practice their typical psychological genocide on everyone which poses no extra effort on their part since they don't believe in a God, heaven or hell for themselves.

Euro-American Caucasian Jews played a significant role in the African slave trade, owning many of the slave ships and were some of the major architects in the drafting of the slave trade business. European Caucasian Jews being at the realm of America's economic controls and subsequent political influence are rendered preferential treatment by government and municipalities on absolutely every level.

The prevalence of Islam in America represents a threat to the control Euro-American Caucasian Jews have maintained in America and through out the world. Euro-American Caucasian Jews are not a spiritual force but instead represent a political and economic force worldwide and move aggressively without any reservations to defend their corporate and class interest in America. They control US financial institutions, media, legal and educational institutions and every facet of American society and a similitude to the state of affairs in Germany just prior to Hitler's persecution and attempted extermination of them. European Caucasian Jews that were persecuted and exterminated by Hitler were not targeted for Hitler's atrocities because of their religion; they were targeted for genocide because of their Caucasian differential ethnicity.

They are European Caucasian people just like the Germans that persecuted them but a different breed as was the same case for the **Roma "Gypsies".**

Between 1933 and 1945 **Roma ("Gypsies")** suffered severely as victims of Nazi persecution and genocide. The Nazi regime viewed Gypsies both as "asocials" (outside "normal" society) and as racial "inferiors" believed to threaten the biological purity and strength of the "superior Aryan" race.

During World War II, the Nazi's and their collaborators killed tens of thousands of **Sinti and Roma** men, women and children across German-occupied Europe. Of these groups of victims of German persecution and extermination the European Caucasian Jews were the only ones to demand and receive compensation payment for the atrocities inflicted upon them.

The apology and payment settlement for the Holocaust placed Jews in American heaven immediately while their block unity and immovable organization gained world wide respect but mainly that of America. The pace at which Islam is growing in America and through out the world threatens the stronghold American Caucasian Jews have on major American economic events and products such as; Christmas and other profit generating commercial holidays.

These are the people who control and direct African American dollars, have strategically and successfully dissolved African American culture and shut down African American socio political and economic movement.

The pork industry had already experienced financial arduous strains with the discontinued consumption of pork products by African American younger generations, and now given the rapid growth of the religion of Islam in America, the pork industry like other industries suffering economic straits could conceivably go out of business. Though Jews are forbidden the consumption and any use of pork products, they maintain ownership and major investments in the pork industry.

Probably the majority of Islamic conversions among African American men transpire in jails behind prison walls and in ways similar to that of the late great and iconic Malcolm X. Jails for young African American men are the unfortunate institutions set up as part of a maze where mostly, Black male individuals are perpetually tricked into walking into their own confinement and surrendering their minute liberties and freedom. This is the place where inmate individuals are forced to become as hostile as their environments for the sake of survival and only few things make since to them, for most incarcerated African American young men, Islam and the oneness of Allah, represents that since able intervention and enlightenment.

13.   Incarceration Instead of Education

Prison-industrial complex

Herod the Great, the king of Judea, gave orders to murder all male babies of the age of two and under in Bethlehem and the vicinity to avoid the rise of a messiah.

The newly fast paced pervasive trend and serious problem of drug peddling, gun toting and murder became the focal point of police departments throughout the country requiring them to implement their random "stop and frisk", one of the main elements of martial law.

"Stop and frisk" would increase the number of African American incarcerations and enhance the need for the expansion of Prison-industrial complex.

Prison-industrial complex (PIC) is a term used to attribute the rapid expansion of the US inmate population owing to the political influence of private prison companies and businesses that supply goods and services to government prison agencies. The term is analogous to the military-industrial complex that President Dwight D. Eisenhower warned of in his famous 1961 farewell address.

Such groups include corporations that contract prison labor, construction companies, surveillance technology vendors, lawyers, and lobby groups that represent them. Activists have described the prison industrial complex as perpetuating a belief that imprisonment is a quick fix to underlying social problems such as homelessness, unemployment, drug addiction, mental illness, and illiteracy.

The promotion of prison building as a job creator and the use of inmate labor are also cited as elements of the prison industrial complex. The term often implies a network of actors who are motivated by making profit rather than solely by punishing or rehabilitating criminals or reducing crime rates. Proponents of this view believe that the desire for monetary gain has led to the growth of the prison industry and the number incarcerated individuals. These views are often shared by people who fear or condemn excessive use of power by government, particularly when related to law enforcement and military affairs.

Racial profiling had already been in effect without an official title sense slaves were officially granted freedom after the civil war.

The worst part of racial profiling "stop and frisk" policy is the allowance of police to stop absolutely anyone even without suspect ion, which translates into African American males, particularly the younger generation. Statistically most African American men stopped were not in possession of illegal drugs or weapons of any sort on their persons nor the subjects of outstanding warrants and were usually law abiding citizens without criminal histories or records, this created a stigma amongst all African American men creating in them the stigmatized feeling of "suspect and guilt based on race classification".

In July of 2010 in the State of New York, Governor David Paterson signed into legislation a law discontinuing the storage in data banks of information obtained from persons stopped and frisked randomly by police. This new legislation is not the end of "stop and frisk" only an end to its data banks. Many African Americans expressed that this bill addressed the wrong issues leaving Black men perhaps now more vulnerable to random "stop and frisk" with added retaliation from racist law enforcement agencies in the form of increased "stop and frisk" harassments and cause African American citizens to question if this was our best attempt in concerted efforts with the first African American governor of the State of New York. Ironically weeks after the new legislation was singed into law by Governor Patterson the states new statistics on "Stop and frisk" were released showing that in just the first half of the year the number of Black and Hispanic men had already exceeded the years total for the previous year by two per cent.

Gang culture was as American as apple pie and stems further back than the Jesse James train Robbery's and the later on Al Capone era's though mangled perception would have many believe it began with the "Bloods and Cripps".
America's real concern with gangs such as the Bloods, Cripps and any youthful group of Black men dissatisfied with the injustices perpetrated against them and their people by a evil racist society and government is as Minister Malcolm X so profoundly warned and explained, "The African American youth of the future will have very little or no compromise in them at all".

The Mafia, one of America's most prominent gangs played a major role in the development of the US economy with its conspirator influence in politics, religion and control of most illegal economically profitable entities such as gambling, alcohol, drugs and guns. Italian criminal societies appeared in the 1800s and became known as the Mafia. They infiltrated the social and economic fabric of Italy and now impact the world. They are some of the most internationally notorious and widespread of all criminal societies. There are several groups currently in the US; the Sicilian Mafia; the Camorra or Neapolitan Mafia; the Ndrangheta or Calabrian Mafia; and the Sacra Corona Unita or United Sacred Crown. Numerous illegal Mafia operations existed in African American communities with full control by African Americans and ownership by Mafia who were parasites deliberately obstructing the progress of African American people for their own self economic advancement. Because of their influences in law enforcement, the Mafia was able to take over any organized profitable activity in African American communities, weather legal or not.

A very real and true example of their influence was witnessed in the takeover of the illegal numbers business which began in Harlem, New York. An African American woman created the concept in order to provide another way for Black folk to acquire economic resources.

Another, of many clear cut cases, where necessity is the mother of adventure; led African Americans to illegal resources to offset their economic denials.

Black crime in America usually involved traditional vices such as; thievery, gambling, prostitution and robbery. Bolito (the numbers game) and drugs became key factors in the evolvement of Black organized crime during the 1920s and 1930s. By 1925 there were thirty Black policy banks in Harlem, several of them large enough to collect bets in an area of twenty city blocks and across three or four avenues. More than 800 runners (bet collectors) spent each day hurrying back and forth between betting customers and the policy bank (clearing house). Bets could be made throughout Harlem's beauty parlors, bars, restaurants, pool halls, barber shops, drugstores, cleaners, stores and other business establishments. Runners even went to people's homes where they could place bets right at their doorsteps. The Mafia eventually invaded the organization, took it over, and ran the owner and founder out of town. The number business remained in effect enabling Blacks some benefit from it since they provided its market.

The big dilemma concerning guns would eventually become the out of control "Blacks killing Blacks", "Dodge City mentalities and environments that drugs and guns festered.

On a national average it's factual that more White's possess guns than do African Americans, however! The distinct unfortunate and dreadful difference is that Whites don't for the most part shoot each other down on their streets like wild dogs converting their environments into havoc, hostile communities.

In American Democracy, every American is afforded the constitutional right to bear arms for the protection of his or her person, family and property.

The issue of the Second Amendment is repeatedly bought before the US Supreme Court due to the regulations individual states place on gun possession, the court concluding in its ruling that these state imposed regulations are unconstitutional.

Chicago, Illinois a city currently with probably the nations highest murder rate is a recent testament and example of the US Supreme Court's ruling in favor of citizens rights to own and bear arms.

It's clear and quite evident that the people responsible for the rise in particularly Chicago's violent crimes and escalated murder rate had illegal guns long before the Supreme Court's recent ruling.

In order to save the African American communities from the havoc wreaked by criminal elements within the community, the community must in good conscience unison with objective law enforcement agencies and sincere African American leadership or representatives begin to isolate these toxic threatening elements forcing them to either comply with the dictates of the people of the state and community populace or forego societal expulsion and incarceration. The destructive criminal behavior of those tainting and tarnishing the image and quality of life of the African American community should not result in African American citizens vicariously surrendering any of their meager liberties or extremely limited constitutional rights. When predominately African American communities in cities like Chicago violently spiral out of control as it recently has without any viable remedy, given the latest Supreme Court ruling, should raise serious concerns of eventual martial law implementation.

Unfortunately, African Americans often times find themselves in situations where the devil is actively in the details preventing their productive and positive progress.

There is no question about what the American government's honest consensus is regarding presumptive African Americans exercising their constitutional second amendment right to bear arms. Guns in the hands of African Americans are one of White America's greatest concerns primarily due to fear of possible retaliatory acts against Whites for continuous oppression and systemic injustices perpetrated against Blacks. African Americans killing each other are not a government concern or priority instead the violence, murder and drug behavior that African Americans revel in represents an unfortunate but effective strategic marginalization in American society.

Pathologically African Americans have become comfortable with what is commonly referred to as "Black against Black Crime" and particularly murders. African Americans show very little if any rage when Blacks kill each other but become immediately outraged when police kill Blacks.

Another evident and clear case of shifting in dynamics where African Americans have been tricked or groomed through the centuries to believe that other Blacks were their potential enemies for any number of superficial reasons and since they historically always witnessed the torture of fellow African American people by brutally oppressive whites, it became the African Americans simplistic inherent method for dealing with other African American issues without any concentrated conflict resolve effort. This behavior by whites and blacks is just another of the many issues that have gone un-addressed, un-resolved and have blossomed into a pathological dangerous acceptable norm.

Whites have been killing African Americans for so long that they don't know how to stop and therefore, must by any means be stopped. Their murder of African Americans became an American pastime and Blacks killing each other have become somewhat of a psychotically sensational entertainment.

The government's new concern and concentrated focus is on gentrification as Whites are rapidly migrating from their formerly secluded suburbs to the inner cities throughout the country for modern convince and an upgraded economic advantage, they must be shielded and protected from the threatening image and presence of Blacks by law enforcement agency's that must reset the community standards using forceful methods of antagonism against current African American residents, then instituting and implementing new rules for the benefit of White relocating arrivals.

This change in the pigmentation and economics of Black communities like Harlem and the Harlem's throughout the country has been dramatic and tragic especially for under-privileged African Americans.
To often African Americans don't see the devil's in these deceptive details and once again become frustrated with the congestion of impoverished African American lifestyle and vent their frustrations and anger in ways that bring critical diminishing return to the entire community leaving devastating lasting effects.

Police brutality against African Americans is a component initially built into America's infrastructure with no consequences for racist hate driven behavior of police and became more visible as a result of the camera technology of "Big brother" unintentionally policing the police and in many cases providing images of the most graphic and horrendous acts of assault to human beings with pictures worth thousands of words.
Ironically, in recent decades when Blacks were victims of police brutality and excessive force, their were always African American

police officers present and if not directly involved in executing the vicious criminally inhumane behavior, stood idly by witnessing and officially enabling it to occur. When these Black officers are questioned by civilian complainants, courts and the African American community, they replied like the German Nazi's did regarding the slaughter and persecution of the Jews under Hitler's orders, "I was just doing my job". The rebuttal expressed to the African American communities by African American law enforcement fraternal associations when these atrocities occur is outrage then on to; explanations of how African American men should submissively respond when stopped by police officers to avoid being murdered or victimized with excessive force and brutality.

Ironically, it's extremely rare for police officers to mistakenly kill armed men intending to commit crimes or merely in possession of illegal weapons or drugs and accidental killings of white men by white police officers is almost nonexistent. The Black men that are killed by the excessive force and brutalities of evil racist systemic police practices are in most cases unarmed and still determined to have posed a mysterious unrealistic, un-evident threat and danger to the safety of police officers who in return acted with the application of deadly physical force resulting in death.

Amadou Diallo killed by four N.Y.P.D. plain-clothed officers: Sean Carroll, Richard Murphy, Edward McMellon, and Kenneth Boss on February 4, 1999. The four officers fired a total of 41 rounds at Diallo. All four officers were acquitted at trial in Albany, New York. This was one of many horrific unfortunate examples of perpetually systemic, murderous, evil racist police hate practices.

The first real progressive step toward stopping police brutality is initiating an internal effort by African American police officers to terminate the evil and race hateful white police culturally brute practices against Blacks, then refuse to tolerate and witness the unwarranted illegal brutal attacks and murders against Black people particularly young Black men by police officers.

The second importantly progressive step toward eliminating police brutality against African Americans is the discontinuance of Black police officers demonstrating to their white colleagues by use of the "Willie Lynch" technique; how they are better capable of inflicting effective punishment on their own people and humiliating them for police audience spectators, which requires a reversal in the terms: "former slave and slave master" to be used in the present tense.

Lastly! There must be some alleviation or reduction in impact in the psychological dynamics of the "Bad Boy", "Thug" and Gangster image that seemingly confuses Black police officers causing them to stratle the fence, wanting to be or look like tough "Home Boys" verses the image of conservatively composed and refined police officers. This is another clear example of the "Fractured Identity" disorder that African Americans suffer, and in these instances carry over into the workplace of policing.
The confusion is simply due to American law enforcement agencies representing and maintaining institutions of white supremacy, and inferiority complexes attained in many cases during the intimidated youth of many recruits which resulted in their passively obedient behaviors that ultimately sheltered them from ordinary criminal

behavior elements and qualified them for law enforcement and other bondable jobs. A significant number of male police officers were either physically or psychologically bullied as youth and bring baggages of lingering vendettas to their jobs. Though Black police officers ascertain the "Black Thug Gangster" image to be negative; yet, they ascribe to it because of its tough look and image of sensual masculinity, which is the only way many young Black men know to boost their self esteem and improperly measure manhood. At the end of the work day many of these African American officers struggle to readjust to "Hood Life" and mind set, needing to fit in back on the home front. This psychological malfunction carries over into the work place, emotionally straining the ability of Black police officers to effectively do their jobs.

It's an undisputed sad but clear fact that when African Americans are put in positions of authority they feel the need to attach extra proof to white's of their un-biasness to fellow Blacks, and in many cases, reversibly exercise excessive measures against other Blacks. The socio psychological reason for this conduct is that when Blacks execute any authoritative powers on Whites they must play solely by the written rules, and never be excessive or over zealous in their execution of authority, however! When those same powers are executed on Blacks by fellow Blacks, this provides the executor an opportunity of egotistical sensationalism and gratification when excessively exaggerating their power or authority.
American law enforcement agencies have the added concern of possible retaliation by African Americans legally exercising their constitutional second amendment right, should they suddenly decide to start shooting back at police when they become subject to the

usual police brutality and excessive force practices so often justified by the prevalently racist American judicial system.

African American police officers that witness injustices perpetrated against African Americans by their comrades are essentially a main official element (Accessory) to that crime by allowing it to occur. The fact that African American police officers never mistakenly shoot and kill white citizens speaks to either fear or skill and mere humane consideration.

African American leadership and Black law enforcement fraternal associations must immediately begin to encourage Black officers to shun and deplore any injustices to African American citizens or any people.

Unfortunately, in American society there is an unwritten rule that states that whenever an African American assumes any position of official power or authority they must assure their constituents that they won't in any capacity show or render preferential treatment to African Americans. African Americans then eagerly make every concentrated effort to demonstrate to their constituents, subordinates, superiors and scrutinizers looking on to ensure that African Americans do not benefit from official authoritative positions of Blacks and are in no way empowered by them, Blacks then enthusiastically prove beyond any shadow of doubt that they are un-biased especially to the concerns of their own people. Subsequently many African Americans escape the hostilities of the ghetto life and environment without any future association or significant contributions leaving in the community the emotionally social effects of abandonment and deep economic distress.

The entire equation of African American male incarceration actually spells "incarceration for capital" especially when considering the components of employment and profit obtained by those in pursuit of such economic benefits from a industry that generates billions of dollars, most of which are citizen tax dollars.

The intelligence and greatness of a nation is manifested in the children that that nation produces. It is economically more affordable and certainly advantageous to the future of any nation, to college educate youth than to incarcerate them, a thought only to be entertained by the powers that be, when and if ever, the element of racism is eliminated from the equation.

It cost a minimum of $22,000 per year to keep an inmate in prison.

A cost that is exceeding the prison budgets of many states due to the general rise in cost of living and the continual rapid growth in prison population.

For example: In 2008, 64,620 people were behind bars in New York State, representing a 1.1 drop over the previous year.

In 2009 the total prison population throughout the country was at 2,297,400, of which 1,617,478 were in federal and state prison and 679,992 were in local jails.

New York State spent $3.622 billion in fiscal year 2008 on corrections. The United States has the largest prison population in the entire world and spends more than any other nation to house prisoners.

U.S. incarceration rates by race, June 30, 2006 Whites: 409 per 100,000 Latinos: 1,038 per 100,000 Blacks: 2,468 per 100,000 Routine exercises in American racism have become excessively costly and the business of incarceration is depleting the budgets of many states leaving them to brainstorm for alternatives to incarceration and technological advancements that would be economically more affordable for projected continued prison population increase throughout the nation.

As un-employment rates rise, so do poverty rates, which will certainly double the current prison population and change the racial statistics as the number of whites will be suddenly significantly increased.

14. White Supremacy

The Main Component In Establishing American Imperialism.

While African Americans remain inundated with the perplexing issues of day to day living, thoroughly armed White Militia Supremacist and Ku Klux Klan train and prepare for the take over of American government and war on all non whites.

The notion that Black people are human beings is a relatively new but not totally accepted discovery in the co-called modern western world.

During the course of the struggle of African people against European racism, brutality and domination, many innovative thinkers have risen from our ranks. The greatest and most courageous scholars have devoted their lives to the pursuit of an explanation for the virtually inherent animosity most white people appear to have toward people of color. Unlike her predecessors, Dr. Frances Cress Welsing, a brilliant, psychiatrist has rejected conventional notions about the origin and perpetuation of racism and her theories, lectures and scientific papers have provoked controversy for over twenty years.

Dr. Frances Cress Welsing, States:

"It should be noted that in the majority of instances, any neurotic drive for superiority usually is founded upon a deep and pervading sense of inadequacy and inferiority. Is it not true that white people represent in numerical terms a very small minority of the world's people? And more profoundly, is not "white" itself the very absence of any ability to produce color? I reason, then, that the quality of whiteness is indeed a genetic inadequacy or a relative genetic deficiency state, based upon the genetic inability to produce the skin pigments of melanin (which is responsible for all skin color). The vast majority of the world's people are not so afflicted, which suggest that color is normal for human beings and color absence is abnormal. Additionally, this state of color absence acts always as a genetic recessive to the dominant genetic factor of color production. Color always "annihilates" (phenotypically-and genetically-speaking) the non-color, white. Black people possess the greatest color potential, with brown, red and yellow peoples possessing lesser quantities, respectively. This is the genetic and psychological basis for The Cress Theory of Color-Confrontation and Racism (White Supremacy).

The Color-Confrontation theory states that the white or color-deficient Europeans responded psychologically, with a profound sense of numerical inadequacy and color inferiority, in their confrontations with the majority of the world's people-all of whom possessed varying degrees of of color-producing capacity. This psychological response, whether conscious or unconscious, revealed an inadequacy based on the most obvious and fundamental part of their being, their external appearance. As might be anticipated in terms of modern psychological theories, whites defensively developed an uncontrollable sense of hostility and aggression. This attitude has continued to manifest itself throughout the history of mass confrontations between whites and people of color. That the initial hostility and aggression came only from whites is recorded in innumerable diaries, journals and books written by whites. Also, records indicate that only after long periods of great abuse have no-whites responded defensively with any form of counterattack. This perplexing psychological reaction of whites has been directed towards all peoples with the capacity to produce melanin. However, the most profound aggressions have been directed towards Black people, who have the greatest color potential and, therefore, are the most envied and feared in genetic color competition."

The idea of African American equality in beauty, culture and intellectual capacity remains problematic and controversial within prestigious halls of learning and sophisticated intellectual circles resulting in internalized White Supremacy and commonly manifesting itself specifically in the exploitation of lighter skin complexion in Black people.

The African American encounter and experience with the western world has clearly been shaped by the doctrine of white supremacy which is embodied in American institutional race hate practices.

Militia is a word of Latin derivative, meaning; military, a term describing any number of groups in the US. The early colonialist of America considered the militia an essential social structure, necessary to provide defense and public safety, also described as a group of white American citizens ready to fight in any emergency. Immediately following the Civil War, the role of policing the southern states fell upon provisional Militia units of former Rebel confederate soldiers. Their activities were terrororistic and aimed directly at Negroes (African Americans) who displayed a tendency to assert their newly granted freedom and independence.

Their vicious and hateful racist evils enabled them to kill "Four little Girls in Alabama".

The 16th Street Baptist Church bombing was an evil racially motivated terrorist attack on September 15, 1963, by committed members of the Ku Klux Klan group in Birmingham, Alabama in the United States.

The bombing of the African American church resulted in the deaths of four innocent little girls. In the early morning of Sunday, September 15, 1963, Bobby Frank Cherry, Thomas Blanton, Herman Frank Cash, and Robert Chambliss, members of the United Klans of America, a Ku Klux Klan group, planted a box of dynamite with a time delay under the steps of the church, near the basement. At about 10:22 am, when twenty six children were walking into the basement assembly room for closing prayers of a sermon entitled "The Love That Forgives," the bomb exploded. The sermon never took place because of the bombing explained Denise McNair's father.

Four little girls, Addie Mae Collins (aged 14), Denise McNair (aged 11), Carole Robertson (aged 14), and Cynthia Wesley (aged 14), were killed in the attack, and 22 additional people were injured, one of whom was Addie Mae Collins younger sister, Sarah.

This was just one of the historically later but quite notable, of the numerous vicious and incensed racist attacks against African Americans by the Ku Klux Klan. National outrage at abuses like this by provisional militia led to their disbandment on March 2, 1867 only to unofficially and illegally revamp strengthening their violent supremacist ideology, recruitment and anger.

The Klan have infiltrated America's mainstream government and law enforcement agencies penetrating everywhere from Central Intelligence Agencies (C.I.A.), Federal Bureau of Investigation (F.B.I.) and political arenas to local police departments in African American communities. The Klan was initially a product of the confederate south following the civil war, the Ku Klux Klan emerged to suppress and victimize freed slaves. They spread throughout the south as an insurgent movement after the civil war and became known as a secret white nationalist vigilante group.

The words "Ku Klux Klan" are onomatopoetic words for the sounds of loading and locking a bolt-action rifle. The Klan objectively seeking a totalitarian state that will control every facet of American life traded their traditional white hoods and robes in for suits, ties, police uniforms and judge robes and then disciplined themselves to be able to work and stand side by side unequivocally with any of their enemies to achieve their ultimate objective.

White militia supremacist on the other hand, vehemently refuses to stand by non Whites in any capacity while they attempt to achieve any level of progress. They teach and train their children early on, the importance of White supremacy and power in America.

They engage their young children in war games to expertly enhance their weaponry and military skills. They imbed in the minds of their youth, superiority and entitlement! America belongs to them exclusively, and a notion that any progress made by non whites especially African Americans is a threat to the sustainability of their white supremacist America. Both of these white supremacist groups are concentrated mainly in western and Midwestern states but do not limit themselves or their activities to those areas.

The general passionate emphasis that white Americans place on "Their Country" when referring to America is quite interesting if one took specific notice. It's a passion that's only necessarily expressed when the gains are ill gotten which in turn produces an inherent fear that they may be taken away the same way. Only sadistic evil can speak without remorse for nations (tribes) of Native Americans exterminated in order to have their own land taken away from them in order to establish a Euro-American white supremacist empire. White America is a classic example of how hateful and demonic a people can become and not even realize the intensity of their evil since they can't objectively see any fault in themselves and have behaved in their evil manor for many centuries with a hate-filled consistency. White Americans have become one with the evils that they've created, entertained, imitated, and practiced throughout their Euro-American history.

A racial and socio economic paradigm shows the acceptability by American society for whites to posses and bear fire arms yet clearly unacceptable for the same of African Americans. Guns represent the ultimate in self-defense; therefore, any adversary would be reasonably concerned with his opposition's ability to level the playing field by possessing equal might.

15.   New World Order

A Day Of Denial And Regret For America

The great conflict of Gog and Magog. Gog and Magog shall be turned loose! Gog and Magog is the divine promise of the ultimate truth.

The barrier that was made to hold the depredations of Gog and Magog will crumble and they will take possession of every point of vantage and convenience, so as to dominate the whole world.

It's an evil wind that blows no good! And an evil genius that goes the way the evil wind blows.

The 21st century is a time of global racial activity when each group of human beings must exercise its own initiative and influence for its own interest and protection, therefore, African Americans should be more concerned and determined today than they've ever been, due to the mighty forces of the world that are operating against non-organized groups of people, who aren't ambitious enough to establish and protect their own interests. America's future becomes dire and bleak with the installation of the New World Order.

The term "New World Order" was frequently used by Adolph Hitler and in more recent times, used by President; George W. Bush II.

New World Order is the globalization of world governments and economies. Globalists adhere to the old Illuminati philosophy of "The end justifies the means." A main and very significant part of Globalists agenda is to create a centralized bank, one headed by a succession of elitists who would unconstitutionally control America's money and its economy for decades. This is not a conjured conspiracy theory though the facts within the context of the subject might be frightful, thus, leading one to think so. There are many answers and abundant information in the silence of the subject of New World Order.

In conspiracy theory, the term New World Order refers to the emergence of a bureaucratic collectivist one-world government.

The conspiracy theory about New World Order is that secretive power elite with a globalist agenda is conspiring to eventually rule the world through an authoritarian world government, which replaces sovereign nation-states, and an all-embracing ideology, which indoctrinates cosmopolitanism.

Significant occurrences in government politics and finance are speculated to be orchestrated by an extremely influential cabal operating through secret political gatherings and decision-making processes. Prior to the early 1990s New World Order conspiracism was limited to two American countercultures, primarily the military anti-government right, and secondarily fundamentalist Christians concerned with end-time emergence of the Antichrist.

New World Order establishment became a process requiring world leadership revamping and the start would be in the United States of America, then on to Iraq and Afghanistan and unequivocally the Vatican in Rome, Italy, installing a Pope whom interestingly and coincidently grew up as a German Nazi, Pope Benedict XVI.

Former president George W. Bush has been accused of being a war monger and cause of the US down turn in economy. If the accusations were valid he would certainly deserve the blame and though they are inaccurate he indirectly and pompously accepts the blame which gives him the desired and much needed image of competence he would not have achieved as the lame and incompetent president he was about to become had there not been the conspired and orchestrated antics and atrocities of 911. He was a man almost pathetically clueless to the magically mechanical workings of American government and inherited his father's unfinished classified business of war for oil confiscation in the Middle East and Afghanistan. His father George Bush Sr. was once CIA director and eventually elected to a one term US presidency of which the second Persian Gulf War was born and ended February 28, 1991.

In 1980 Iraq and Iran were at war with each other until 1988 and that war was often refereed to as the Persian Gulf War. America planned her conflicts in the Middle East decades ago and attempted to prepare Americans for such invasions through American media in the form of movies such as the 1986 movie "Iron Eagle" Directed by: Sidney J. Furie, and starring: Louis Gossett Jr., Jason Gedrick and David Suchet.

"True Lies" Directed by: James Cameron, starring: Arnold Schwarzenegger, Jamie Lee Curtis and Tom Arnold.

These movies clearly depicted decades in advance staged events that would ultimately take place between the United States and oil producing Middle Eastern countries, deliberately created and designed to change the image of an entire race of people from devoutly religious to internationally terrorist.

The Middle East, (a term coined by the US military during WWII applying to a region,) is comprised of Muslim countries, all of which until recently were theocracies, (governments controlled by divine or religious laws) Islamic Law.
America with feelings of imperialistic entitlement, tyranny, thirst and greed for oil planned and calculated decades ago her eventual invasions of oil producing Middle Eastern countries with clear intentions to humiliate the people, ravage the land, confiscate the oil and forcefully impose an American version of democracy. America was in need of an effectively unique strategy that would ascertain her justification for tyrannical futuristic invasions and attacks on countries refusing to give her the oil she desired and demanded.

911 was masterfully conspired and created with the devil in the details two years before its actual implementation and the needed death toll required determining an act of war was committed against America. A previous attempt was made on blowing up the World Trade Center but foiled.

Because of America's militaristic and imperialistic design, designated enemies, foreign and domestic are necessary for the "Oligarchy" American system to work.
"Oligarchy" is defined as a government in which a small group exercise control for corrupt and selfish purposes.

Modern wars are generally the outgrowth of dissatisfied capitalistic interests among foreign people of other nations.

Until a universal adjustment takes place the State or Nation should have the power to conscript and use without any obligation to repay, the wealth of such individuals or corporations through whose investments or interests, in foreign countries, or among foreign peoples wars are fomented and made; in which the nation is called upon to make sacrifices in men, money and other resources, as is generally done in times of war, and those most interested or responsible by their acts of selfishness go free, or only bear but a proportionate part of the burden.

The entire burden of the war should rest upon and be the responsibility of those whose interests brought about the difficulties, and they should be made to pay the full cost of such wars.

People like the Rockefeller's, Rothschild's, Firestone's, Sinclair's, and so on, should not be allowed to entangle the nation in foreign disputes, leading to war, for the sake of satisfying their personal, individual or corporate selfishness and greed for more wealth at the expense of the innocent masses of both countries.

Oil "concessions" in the Middle East; sugar or coffee "concessions" in Haiti, West Indies, or any where else to be exploited for selfish enrichment of individuals, sooner or later, end in disaster; hence ill-feelings, hate and then war.

The well known trick of the selfish capitalists is to stir up local agitation among the designated nations; have them shoot or kill some citizen of the capitalist's country, and then he influences the agencies of his government to call upon the home authorities for protection.

A harsh diplomatic note is sent that inspires an insult of further injury, then an ultimatum is served or a demand made for indemnities or war declared with the hope of arresting from the particular weak, unfortunate country such as territories where oil, valuable minerals and other natural resources are to be found.

The illegal wars that America engages in today are once again a clear result of the power of the wealthy owners of the American private banking systems. This type of conspiracy practice is born of the structural dynamics in capitalism and known as dollar diplomacy.

In America corporations are now being made to legally equal that of citizens for the enhancement of corporate greed which will ultimately aid in America's demise.

The event of 911 was something Americans could not fathom; an attack on American soil was inconceivable to the world and especially Americans before it actually happened. America usually does the attacking, dropping her bombs on other countries, killing its inhabitants then leaving and returning home to a country always safe and secure from any retaliation from foreign victims of American attacks and invasions.

TERORISM! TERRORISM! TERRORISM! TERRORISM!

The term, label and constant re-iterations of the word "Terrorist" are a significant strategic element for effective physical and psychological warfare and a convenient periodic distraction.

This time because America had inevitably entered into a global economy the nature of which was time sensitive, the stakes were extremely higher and all wagers were placed on the table ready for the switch to be flicked for the official implementation of the New World Order.

America's 911 masterminds had no qualms with the projected numerous American casualties that would result from an attack on the World Trade Center and US Pentagon.

America being an expert in foreign intelligence and having extensive experience in a vast range of domestic and foreign intelligence operations including everything from toppling governments, creating cue's, and actual all out wars, leaves very little question about her prior knowledge or involvement in the diabolic creation and implementation of 911.

For many Americans especially those of various official government status, the implementation of the New World Order by way of 911 was secretly viewed as a success giving America a free pass to invade countries under the guise that the specified Muslim countries harbored terrorist.

Though America concluded that the alleged terrorist who presumably perpetrated the attacks against the United States were from Saudi Arabia, Saudi Arabia was clearly not to be held responsible nor accountable for the actions of her fellow countrymen.

America and Saudi Arabia have been in bed together for an extended period of time sharing in common; special interest in the business of oil, wealth and international prestige greatly influenced and encouraged by America. In fact government classified information was recently leaked and confirmed stating; that Saudi Arabia has been pleading and begging America to militarily attack Iran.

Most Americans knew nothing or very little of American foreign policy or the American involvement in the war between Afghanistan and Soviet Marxist repression which failed but of which the Taliban was created by the United States, Central Intelligence Agency (C.I.A.).

America invaded Afghanistan to dismantle their theocratic ally political autonomy and install an American democratic system which would enable them to reap the rich resource of the country.

War at this current date and time in America's history translates into big profits as wars generally do. America has declined from being sovereign, and the leading industrious powerful nation she was once internationally known to be and replaced her production of natural goods with the production of wars and war products. The creation and business of war has become the world's number one commodity though many Americans are concerned that America's fight in Afghanistan may convert into a similitude to that of the Soviet's who were forced to retreat and return home to a collapsed government.

The Soviet's with their military might and advanced weaponry which is believed to be significantly more advanced than American weaponry were still no match for the Afghanis and mountainous warfare which leads one to wonder what's in store for the Americans.

Drugs have become a significant product of modern war generating billions of dollars throughout the economies of many countries.

When the Soviet's left Afghanistan they left with immeasurable weight of heroin which flooded the streets of the Soviet Union creating a heroin drug epidemic and immorally giving some financial stimulation to their weakened economy at the same time, which was critically needed due to the immediate collapse of government the Soviet Union experienced when withdrawing from their war with Afghanistan.

Drugs are aggressively and securely obtained from poppy growing countries like Afghanistan in almost the same ways that oil is swindled from oil producing countries.

Two main popularly demanded products with immeasurable profit.

America has had her majestic day, Super power for approximately sixty five years beginning after World War II, and now her race seems to be inevitably to the bottom as capitalism dangles with desperation, nearing the verge of defeat, and China prepares to take America's resentful place as a Super Power of a new and different magnitude. The installation of New World Order eliminates the need, use or previous power of the United States Constitution as New World Order is a global entity comprised of every nation in the world playing a different but very significant part.

The New World Order is perceived by some to be a last ditch effort to "Save the World" or "Save some from a failing world". The climate produced in America and throughout the world as a result of installing New World Order is one of civilian unrest, chaos, confusion and pandemonium.

Americans without conscious realization will give up their liberties gradually and willingly under almost no direct pressure.

A clear and unfortunate example of this willingness to render ones liberties is the volatile case in New York City where a controversial nationwide conversation has sparked following the proposal of a Muslim-themed community center and Mosque two blocks from Ground Zero.

The opposition harbors the national pain of the aftermath of the alleged terrorist attacks on September 11 and expressionlessly feels it is insulting and insensitive to the families and memory of the nearly 3,000 victims including Muslims that lost their lives. On the other side of the issue, religious freedom is decreed in the US constitution, therefore, developers of the Park 51 Islamic Cultural Center have a legal right or status to build wherever they desire.

In the Pentagon, which was also subject to the terrorist attack on September 11, there is a non-denominational center where Muslims regularly pray throughout the week and hold "Jumma" (Friday assembly prayer) services on Fridays.

Imam Al-Hajj Talib Abdur-Rashid of the Mosque of Islamic Brotherhood Inc. In Harlem, New York in an interview with the Amsterdam News, August 26-September 1, 2010 issue.

"Imam-Rashid sees and expresses something missing when it comes to the national conversation: Black Muslims".

"The first thing we need to do is decode some of the language," said Imam Abdur-Rashid.

"The first language that has to be decoded is "Americans". That really means "white Americans". That's who's really uptight about this.

"The opposition that is coming from certain segments of the white American community is not just tied to the building of mosques.

There's a race angle", he said. Ethnicity wise, it's not just Arabs. Its Arabs and southern Asians.

Southern Asian immigrants, according to all the studies done over the past 15 to 20 years, are the largest group of Muslims in the United States. Then African Americans are second and Arabs are third. The question is asked, why aren't Blacks included in the conversation on Islam? The answer according to Imam Rashid is two-fold.

"The way that this whole issue is playing out is the result of what I call a failed strategy on the part of Arab and southern Asian Muslims to be accepted into American society or assimilation into American society and a successful strategy on the part of the status quo (and) ruling class on the other hand."

Imam Abdur-Rashid believes that the failed strategy of the Arab and southern Asian Muslims was in not promoting a dialogue with Black Muslims once they arrived in America, especially after the Civil Rights act of 1965 and the Immigration Act of 1965.

"An important part of their assimilation strategy has been to put an immigrant face on Islam in America," said Imam Abdur-Rashid.

"Many of the immigrants who have come here have been financially well off. This has enabled them to found influential national organizations as they pursue a strategy of empowerment. All immigrants want to be empowered; all immigrants want to be a part of American society. They've worked to put an immigrant face on Islam in America. "As these immigrants have come here, two things have happened. One is that their goal has been to assimilate into white America, since we all know that there is two Americas. And the America that these southern Asian and Arab immigrants have strived to assimilate to is not the America you and I are sitting in right now," said Imam Abdur-Rashid. "In doing this, the fact is that they came to this country and, for the most part, ignored the presence of African-American Muslims.

(They) made no attempt to link with us, work with us, dialogue with us.

"Up until the past couple of decades, when you said Islam and Muslims in America, people have always thought about African-Americans.

All of the famous Muslims in America up until this decade have been African-Americans who have had tremendous impact on American society.

Malcolm X, Muhammad Ali, Kareem-Abdul Jabbar. The list goes on.

"It's failed not because these same Muslims had ill intent towards African-Americans; it was because they didn't know the territory," Imam Abdur-Rashid continued. "They underestimated the underbelly of American society and the role that racism toward people of color has always played in American society.

After September 11, their artificial white privilege was revoked and they just became another kind of nigger in America. And the status quo started treating them like that."

Muslims are vigorously expressing their determination to exercise their constitutional right to build a Mosque near Ground Zero but unfortunately, need to take an important look at the history of African American people and how the United States Constitution they speak of never played out for the benefit of African Americans, and be reminded that up to this president day in the 21st century in America, African Americans are not protected nor benefactors of the US constitution. Immigrant Muslims must realize that like African Americans, Muslims and the religion of Islam is clearly repulsed, un-welcomed and not admired in America, and racist white Americans have found sanctuary for their ordinary hatred and evils in the Park 51 Mosque project.

This understanding should give immigrant Muslims simplistic clarity and significantly more insight into what African American Muslims have previously endured in order to worship Allah in America, and what they currently endure to maintain their obedience to Allah in a country dismissive to any religion not containing an American Christian composition, and in spite of the clannish separation and distance of immigrant Muslims.

This does not mean nor suggest that Muslims or any other people in the midst of America should surrender their battle for justice and equality, but these various discriminating oppositions should serve as a valuable reminder and lesson on the subject of Muslim unity regardless of ethnicity.

Immigrant Muslims knowing of the suffering and continuous oppression of African Americans and African American Muslims should serve as reason enough to discontinue UN-ISLAMIC and UN-RIGHTOUS practice of insensitivity and indifference to them.

Immigrant Muslim leaders went as far as equating the Park 51 controversy with Rosa Parks (Mother of the Civil Rights Movement) and the Civil Rights movement against Jim Crow.

Jim Crow Laws were state and local laws in the United States enacted between 1876 and 1965. They mandated racial segregation in all public facilities, with supposedly "separate but equal" status for African Americans. This led to treatment and accommodations that were usually inferior to those provided for white Americans, systematizing a number of economic, educational and social advantages.

Muslims attempting to build an Islamic center a few blocks from Ground Zero, where the World Trade Center once stood are being confronted with extreme opposition from Americans from every race, political and religious persuasion imaginable. They have become entangled in the American evil racism circuit which has gone as far as threatening to blow up any Mosque built on the disputed site.

The site of the controversy is currently being used as a Mosque and has been for a several years with no previous attention drawn to it for any reason. What the opposition seem to agree on is the right of Muslims to build a Mosque, but just not at that location.

This argument is supported by Governor David Paterson of New York State and many other citizens.

President Oboma initially sited the constitutional right to build a house of worship wherever desired and available then back peddled a day later expressing uncertainty because of the controversy over the location of the Islamic center to be built.

Interestingly, New York City Mayor M. Bloomberg supported the right to build the Islamic Center at the designated site though prominent American Caucasian Jewish organizations opposed.

Once the right to worship when and where one pleases are unlawfully and unconstitutionally obstructed it raises serious concern for freedom of religion and especially for Caucasian Jews as they historically know from first hand experience where and what the second hand might end up in.

Bilal R. Muhammad

A classic new example for Caucasian Jews to take serious note of; was just months after the Park 51 project controversy erupted, members of the Kansas-based Westboro Baptist Church were screaming messages of what's always considered ant-Semitic hate in front of a Midwood Jewish school in Brooklyn, New York on Monday October 11, 2010.

The white members of the fundamentalist church sang songs and waved signs telling Jews, "Your Doom is coming!" for more than thirty minutes outside Yeshiva Rabbi Chaim Berlin on Avenue I and E. 13th Street, one of three stops in a daylong hate rally.

The fringe church billed its arrival as the Godsmack Tour, a reminder to Jews that the vast majority of them "will be cast into everlasting fire in hell." The church has a website named "godhatesfags.com.

The bigotry, hate and antagonism that have begun with the Muslims certainly won't end with them but will spread across the board of all non-whites and Jews.

Victory for the opposition to the new Islamic Center will mean the setting of a new precedence for where people are allowed to worship relinquishing their liberties which might be inevitable in the New World Order.

In Staten Island, New York, Muslims were engaged in a real estate bind with the New York Arch Dioceses to purchase a former convent to be converted into a Mosque, the neighboring people and politicians opposed the sale pressuring the Catholic Dioceses to withdraw from their contractual bind.

These are just a few more of the many similar incidents throughout the country and some of the many wicked ingredients needed for the recipe of civil unrest or civil and race war.

America is a country that was founded on conspiracy, invasion, slavery, corruption and murder of which her wealth and power was born.

As police states are created throughout the country they rid the country of visual low to mid level corruption which has proven during the process of eradication to contribute to America's economic undoing. Police states enhance civil unrest creating the need for martial law as they direct their focus on quality of life issues rather than the typically usual criminal actions and behaviors. "Police State" methods are used . . . to suppress African American people's honest and just struggle against discrimination and other forms of oppression.

The quality of life issues are simply providing protection for whites and whatever wealth they might have secured or maintained and ensuring their quality of life is shielded from Blacks.

In communities throughout America, Whites are policed for the purpose of ensuring their overall protection, while Blacks are policed to ensure that they are not committing crimes.

General public safety that law enforcement is supposed to provide is not afforded to Blacks on a general practice.

As the American economy worsens with joblessness, poor unemployed people can't pay taxes which clearly means and translates into less revenue for government and problematically severe unemployment which spells a down turn in the national economy overall.

Crime and America was originally a bond that went hand in hand from the out start, crime converted into abundance of money or wealth.

America has evolved into the global economy and New World Order of which the rules are not and will not be American Constitution but will be New World Order!

The American media will subliminally revoke democracy, and the constitutional rights and liberties from American citizen's right before their very eyes without their conscious awareness of what is actually taking place until they arrive at a sudden realization of the gradual change that was taking place the entire time. Installation of New World Order will unequivocally be televised media controlled, and will be played out right before your very eyes. The American media will continue as it currently does, control what people think and what messages are released to create any desired effect. Where people use to make the news, the news now makes the people. The American media is going to be the death of individual intellect.

America has gone from; "We the People" to We the Government and has actively entered the New World Order.

The term "New World Order" presents its self as a topic that when mentioned to most Americans regardless of their backgrounds silences them due to its original historical connection to societal secrecy.

African Americans being the victims of the greatest conspiracy against human beings and constant oppression from that conspirator live with a suspicion of the oppressor knowing his evil potential and capabilities probably better than anyone out side of himself.

Many Americans feel and agree that the gradual implementation of a police state is the actual stage setting for things to come, though they patriotically prefer to not think in terms of conspiracy. African Americans on one hand, will likely be the least directly effected by the non-libertarian policies of New World Order since the American

Constitution never played out fully for them resulting in their having no major investments or representation in America's most major corporations, in essence have very little to lose in the way of capital or material assets and have been conditioned to endure and survive the worst of situations and conditions, however, on the other hand, the un-rehearsed dilemma of New World Order will pose un-affordable and un-sustainable strains on an extremely fragile African American people who must place themselves in a position to contribute to the solidification and establishment of world globalization for the survival and sustainability of the impaired African and African American race.

The African American initial arrival in America is the absolute result of the greatest form of conspired tyranny, terrorism and actual terrorist ever known to man and no one knows the evil capabilities and demonic intentions of white Americans better than African Americans.

The recent revolutionary turmoil in Egypt and Libya is diluting the popularity of American chants of Terrorism.
While America preoccupies herself with her inherent evils of White supremacy, tyranny and thirst to kill millions of human beings throughout the world in the name of an alleged crusade to prevent terrorism, the 21st century will inevitably go to the country that is best able to give its people and the people of the world the leadership and essentials needed to advance world civilization.
There is resentful concern but no doubt that that country is China with her fast paced technological advancements and abundant accumulation of global wealth including enormous international debt

owed to China by countries such as: The United States of America and other significantly economically strained nations throughout the world.

America maintained her status of sovereignty and independence for many years, recently diminishing it, partly due to excessive international debt calculating into the several trillions of dollars which not only relinquishes sovereignty, but also creates added concern to America's national security.

The communist leadership that came to power in 1949 has launched China on the path of modern economic growth within a socialist framework and since has caused China to be recognized as a potential new world leader.

16.   African American Presidents

John Hanson

African Americans can and should pride themselves in knowing of some of the great political contributions made to American society by African Americans during the formative years of the United States of America and John Hanson was just another significant political figure amongst the many.

John Hanson an African American (born in Maryland, April 14, 1721-November 22, 1783) was a merchant and public official from the state of Maryland during the era of the American Revolution.
In 1779 Hanson was elected as a delegate to the Continental of Congress. He signed the Articles of Confederation in 1781 after Maryland finally joined the other states in ratifying them.
In November 1781, he became the first President of Congress to be elected under the terms of the Articles of Confederation.
Mainly white historians reluctantly say that because of this John Hanson is said to be the first President of the United States.
John Hanson is one of the great men conveniently lost in the pages of American history solely due to American racist trifles and nothing to do with intelligence, brilliance and tenacity.

Once the new document (The Articles of Confederation) was drafted, adopted and signed in 1781, a president was needed to run the country.

John Hanson was chosen unanimously by Congress which included George Washington. In fact, all the other potential candidates refused to run against him, due to his being a major player in the revolution and an extremely influential member of congress.

As the first president, John Hanson had precedence to set and an arduous task before him since there hadn't been a president prior to him and the role of president was quite poorly defined.

Six other presidents were elected after John Hanson and prior to George Washington taking office. Ultimately, since the Articles of Confederation didn't work well and the individual states had too much power nothing could be agreed upon which caused the need of a new document to be written, known as the Constitution of The United States.

17.   President Barack Obama

You Can Be The President;
I'd Rather Be The Pope.

You Can Be The Side Effect;
I'd Rather Be The Dope.

Prince

America's final sequel.

Barack Hussein Obama II; (born August 4, 1961) is the 44th and current President of the United States of America.

He is the first African American to hold the office.

President Obama previously served as a United States Senator from Illinois, from January 2005 until he resigned after his election to the US presidency in November 2008.

President Barack Obama successfully won the American presidential election even after the bitter public controversial denunciation of his former pastor Rev. Jeremiah Wright Jr.

Jeremiah Wright Jr. was the pastor of Trinity United Church of Christ, a mega church in Chicago, Illinois exceeding 6,000 members.

Rev. Wright's beliefs and preaching were scrutinized when segments from his sermons were publicized in connection with the presidential campaign of Barack Obama, including his contention that the attacks of September 11, 2001 were proof that "America's chickens are coming home to roost" . . . "Not God Bless America. God damn America".

Barack Obama reacted to the Rev. Wright controversy in a speech entitled "A More Perfect Union."

Rev. Wright subsequently defended himself in a speech before the NAACP on April 27, 2008, in which he indicated that he was not "divisive" but "descriptive," and that the Black church experience, like Black culture, was "different" but not "deficient".

After the election, Rev. Wright was again the center of controversy when he suggested "them Jews" were keeping him from reaching President Obama.

A brilliant, tenacious and charismatic President Obama at first seemed to many Americans as an opportunity for America to redeem herself in the world.

As is circumstance ally usual many African Americans initially believed President Obama's successful election to be a divine gift and intervention from God and had an array of conceptual ideas of what was prosperously in store for African Americans as a result of an African American president.

It later became reluctantly speculative by many African Americans that his presidency would be no more for African Americans than a celebration of symbolism and an honorable mention in the pages of American and African American history.

Almost immediately upon President Obama's assumption of leadership African Americans became a bit confused by the directives of his presidency, thinking that on one hand, the circus had finally left town but were once again stunned and surprisingly disappointed to be reminded that on the other hand, the monkey was still on their backs.

Disappointment and hard times is unfortunately the African Americans oldest friend. African Americans began to feel that they had elected a president that was officially strategically gagged and restrained, relating to African American issues and unable to address the despairing destitute realities of his own people.

The sincerely beloved, adored and respected African American president Obama seemed to have transformed from a redeemer into a manipulated puppet whose strings were being pulled and manipulated by the puppeteers in the persons of the usual evil racist white Euro-American puppet-masters. His charismatic suave and redemptive style initially put African Americans in a cathartic mode that resulted in a growing list of systemic and governing disappointments which made Mr. Obama look less like a president and comically more like the one legged man in the ass kicking contest.

The arrest incident regarding Harvard professor Henry Louis Gates Jr., one of the nations pre-eminent African American scholars, was arrested by Cambridge police investigating a possible break-in which coincidently turned out to be the home of Professor Gates. The incident raised serious concerns among the African American communities that Professor Gates was a victim of racial profiling and the incident prompted a response from president Obama, calling the arresting officers handling of the incident "stupid."

President Obama immediately retracted his initial statement and invited Professor Gates and the arresting police officer to the White House for reconciliation over beer.

Ironically, a few months after this incident, Professor Gates appeared on the Oprah Winfrey show, and explained to the audience that he had researched and discovered that the white officer that had arrested him shared his same DNA, concluding that they were actual relatives. While this delighted Professor Gates, Oprah and her audience, Professor Gates went on to say that his arresting officer and newly discovered blood relative had given him as a souvenir the handcuffs he used in arresting him.

The entire packaged buffoonery sounded every bit, like the patriotism exemplified in happy mis-educated and revised 21st century slaves. This was for the most part a clear cut situation where American white folks reminded President Obama and all Blacks that though Blacks and whites may claim friendships to each other, Blacks will never catch up to whites, even those Blacks with the most prestigious positions.

The presidents back peddling sparked concern among African Americans that the price of an African American president is going to require precise strategy and be in certain ways, quite costly to African Americans leaving them to wonder if having an African American president will be more problematic to African Americans than progressive resolution.

In the state of New York, Governor David Paterson, an African American assumed his governorship as a result of his debunked predecessor, Governor George Pataki and considered running for an elected term as Governor and was discouraged by President Obama who apparently conveniently forgot the over-flow of support he received from people who desired the tenacious talent and diversity he represented but discouraged in others.

Another brilliant African American New York politician known as Bill Thompson ran for mayor of New York City against the current affluent Mayor, Michael Bloomberg who's abundant wealth and socio-political influence enabled him to do away with the two term limits, and was running for a third term, however; Mr. Thompson's campaign was strained because he didn't get the endorsement of his own party member; President Barack Obama.

Through the centuries of slavery and oppression African Americans have seen and experienced more than their share of disappointments and failures by those that have come forward to represent them and though President Obama is not a leader to only African Americans, he inherently reflects the race who want and expect to experience nothing less from his presidency than an everlasting success that will be felt deep in the core of the African American race and history.

Less than a year into his presidency and un-attained significant achievements, President Barack Obama accepts the Nobel Peace Prize with a stern and defensive position of war.

In his acceptance speech President Obama contended that it was still sometimes necessary to go to war. He acknowledged the controversy over the choice of a wartime president for the Nobel Peace Prize and saying he reserved the right to take action to protect the United States.

One of the realities of "$Dollarism" is the obvious transparency of the imperialist who give out Noble Peace Prizes to try to strengthen the image of nonviolence.

After a vicious battle with opponents to President Obama's Hearth Care reform, Mr. Obama emerged victorious.

President Obama signed his landmark health care overhaul bill into law with the strokes of 22 pens.

The Health Care overhaul is the most expansive social legislation enacted in decades.

President Obama had to be jolted and reminded that there was still blood in the water and it wasn't safe to go in while the sharks were swarming around the perimeter.

The accomplishment of Health Care reform and the repeal of Don't Ask, Don't Tell, by President Obama which might very well be his nemesis seemed to ignite and release white racist American hatred and treachery. White Americans viciously pursued President Obama with a vehement disdain he couldn't have imagined would become a reality. Not only did the American White citizens smite him, but republican members of the House of Representatives, moved to repeal his health care reform immediately after winning the house (House of Representatives) back in the mid-term elections.

White America and the American Power Machine, "by way of the American media," once again, began to question his nationality and religion.

The national budget for 2011 reflects federal cuts to close deficits and reduce debt, but will severely hurt African Americans and poor people overall. The recession is still in effect with signs of extremely slow and very sluggish recovery especially in the areas of employment and the housing market.

The mere discontinuation of section 8 housing will devastate the lower income population in America that has depended on its much needed supplementation for many decades.

De-funding of Planned Parenthood and other essential programs like; Home Energy cuts will not only affect Blacks but this time around will significantly effect whites as well.

The proposed cuts outlined in the president's budget have caused Blacks to feel a sense of betrayal by the president. Many African Americans are left to wonder if President Barack Obama truly feels the sufferings, pains and disparities of African American people particularly since he isn't a descendent of slaves.

African Americans cannot fathom that an African American president who developed his political career and character and gained notoriety through community outreach programs would be willing to cut those programs along with other vital programs.

The premise of anyone assuming the presidency of the United States and being a converted or naturalized member of any religion other than Christianity is un-accepted though the American constitution stipulates the afforded freedom of religion for all citizens.

Ironically, while accusations are hurled at President Obama, calling him a Muslim, he; like his predecessor, George Bush, firmly assures America and the world that America is not at war with Islam.

The president's assurances are enormously out weighed by the abundant white American anti-Muslim sentiment.

Many of the young white constituents that vigorously supported President Obama's initial campaign have left his camp lambasting every significant aspect of his administration and joined opposing campaigns to ensure that he won't serve a second term in the White House.

In recently conducted polls numbers reflected that 14% of the American population now thinks President Obama is the Anti Christ.

These and other similar audacious insidious statements are irreversibly tainted by bigotry and hatred.

President Obama's presidency is historically the most difficult and unusual presidency of any American president yet.

Despite the overall disdain and opposition to his ethnicity President Obama resides in the United States presidency during the most transitioning and trying times in the countries history. Certainly, a challenging and testy time in America, when the country is making necessary adjustments to become and maintain their position of partnership in the inevitable new world global revolutionary transition. A distinct era with economic turmoil at a devastating low level and the lengthy war in Afghanistan is beginning to resemble that of the horrific Vietnam War while at the same time America is moving into an inevitable global economy for economic survival.

One of President Obama's frustrating concerns and top priorities is the war in Afghanistan and US withdrawal without a collapse in America's economy which would be a repeat of what happened to the Soviet's upon their withdrawal.

Interesting however, is the fictional sense of confidence that many Americans feel concerning a collapse of American government.

They actually feel it's either impossible or almost impossible for America's government to collapse due to the intervention of economic globalization. It's certainly wishful and optimistic to think that notion is correct and in the event of its inaccuracy, hopefully, America will be spared the possibility of national economic collapse perhaps with the intervention of something else or God.

President Obama inherited a seemingly un-wining war previously attempted by other technologically advanced nations which resulted in their diminishing returns.

As if the wars in Iraq and Afghanistan aren't enough, and before considering the prospects of international sanctions, March 19, 2011 President Obama ordered at least 195 Tomahawk Missile Strikes, against Libyan Leader; Muammar Abu Minyar Al-Gaddafi, aligning himself to become a war criminal like his predecessors, George Bush I and II, both of whom have the innocent death and blood of multi-millions of foreign citizens on their hands as a result of their capitalist gangster behaviors and economic agendas. Though, this is not America's first attempt to topple and oust Gaddafi, President Obama, the British government and America, make the claim that the missile strikes against Libya are necessary to dismantle the Gaddafi regime and deter current Libyan military attacks against ordinary Libyan citizens.

President Obama's contention is that these missile strikes are against Gaddafi supporters and merely serve to aid the rebels and Libyan citizens.

As African Americans analyze the Libyan crisis and America's interest in it we must be encouraged to expand our knowledge of geographical/international politics, then be cautious and cognizant of the un-deniable fact that America is a country who's history is written and drenched in blood, treachery and deceit which simply means; (Holy Qur'an, Chapter, 49. Al-Hujurat v. 6) "O you who believe, if an unrighteous man brings you news, look carefully into it, lest you harm a people in ignorance, and then be sorry for what you did." "The truth needs no help, and a lie don't care who tells it".

Ironically, millions of Africans are killed by various governments, leaders and people throughout the African continent with American and European made weapons and clearly, no concern or intervention from America, which should lead one to wonder what America's real interest is in Libya's internal conflict.

In Rwanda, Africa, 800,000 African people were killed in 100 days and was clearly a severe and critical humanitarian issue with no American or French intervention or cruise missile strikes, in fact America and France immediately went in to extract their citizens while the blood bath continued. America's pretentious concern for innocent African life is absolutely fake and absurd! And never a real issue of concern, if it were, there's millions of despaired and oppressed Africans right here in America.

It should first be noted that Libya is the front line state of the African continent and shares significant responsibility for the establishment of the African Union. Secondly, Libya is an oil rich sovereign nation, and not only a producer of oil, but they produce the best quality of it.

Libya and Nigeria produce the rare and best quality oil called "Body Crude Light".

There's an old saying; "it's the squeaky wheel that gets the oil" and America makes the squeakiest noise over oil.

While Egypt and other Muslim nations are experiencing civil unrest and demanding the replacements of their leadership, America and Britain, might as well pose themselves as the opportunist, they classically are and aid in setting the stage to appease the desire of the western world to re-colonize the African continent. African Americans that weren't already aware, have come to the realization that in order for any one to assume the presidency of the power hungry, blood thirsty United States of America, that person must possess ambitiously corrupt capabilities and certainly represent to some significant degree, Americas impetuous hatred and ill treatment especially, towards African Americans.

A candidate for the presidency of the United States of America must be readily capable of domestic and international tyranny for the benefit of American interest.

For decades, America has maintained a hate relationship with Muammar Gaddafi.

Probably, the saddest aspect to the equation, regarding America's attack against Libya, is what feelings might be contained in the heart of Mr. Obama since he is a direct first generation African descendant with numerous immediate relatives in the country of Kenya, Africa, and the actual birth place of his father. It would serve significant clarity to the African American community if President Obama defined his convictions and until he does the African American people can only assume that he has been enticed, offered and accepted some irresistible package likely entailing wealth he would not have amassed otherwise.

African Americans that are designated to move into positions of power and authority are unfortunately, usually never convinced of the hate and contempt whites maintain for them.

A classic juggling act for Mr. Obama, and masterful multi tasking at the highest level for certain! African Americans share a concern that President Obama has become a victim target of America's supreme form of technical lynching in the sense that he's been strategically set up to represent a disparity and a disappointment to African Americans and America overall. The design of the set up will create delusion and remove future desires of African American trust of other African Americans aspiring positions of leadership regarding the business of running the country or the African American community.

This would certainly become white America's desired sentiment and effectiveness that would unfortunately last among African Americans for many years into the future.

As president Obama winds down a final year in a first term presidency, he must be reminded that he can only play the "African American history card" one time and it's been played.

This might be the ideal time for President Obama to fully practice and exercise his familiarity with the "Audacity of Hope" if he hasn't already begun to do so.

The "Audacity of Hope" is the title of a book written by President Obama. The title of the "The Audacity of Hope" was derived from a sermon delivered by Barack Obama's former pastor, Reverend Jeremiah Wright. Rev. Wright had attended a lecture by Dr. Frederick G. Sampson in Richmond, Virginia, in the late 1980s, on the GF Watts painting Hope, which inspired him to give a sermon in 1990 based on the subject of the painting-"with her clothes in rags, her body scarred and bruised and bleeding, her harp all but destroyed and with only one string left, she had the audacity to make music and praise God . . . To take the one string you have left and to have the audacity to hope".

Having attended Rev. Wright's sermon, Barack Obama later adopted Wright's phrase "audacity to hope" which became his 2004 Democratic Convention Keynote address, and the title of his second book.

History has shown that when African Americans choose their own leaders they most often times unfortunately of the wrong kind. African Americans do not really follow persons with constructive programs. Almost any sort of exciting appeal or trivial matter presented to them may receive immediate attention and temporarily at least liberal support. When the bubble collapses, of course, these same followers will begin to decry Black leadership and call these misrepresentatives of the group rascals and scoundrels.

Inasmuch as they have failed to exercise foresight, however, those who have liberally supported these imposters. Yet the fault here is not inherently in the African American but in what he has been taught.

18. The Final Hour

African Americans Still See What They Want And Desire Through Eyes That Are Blind.

The final hour, is the hour that all the Prophets of Allah, (god) and great men and women of wisdom and vision, foretold and warned would inevitably come to pass, and today is the dreadful day of that final hour with African Americans asking the "rhetorical" question, what do we do in the final hour?

Allah (God) has always sent prophets, preachers and divine men of wisdom to the oppressed people of the earth to repair their torn and despaired conditions, however, their conditions can only be repaired if they heed Allah's (God) call, warning and instructions. The preachers usually tell the people the things they want to hear while the prophets tell the people what they urgently need to hear. The destruction or survival of African American people hinges on "if, and how", our positive creative thoughts transform into actions, and how those actions unfold.

Holy Qur'an CH. 16 V. 77

Ana the matter of the Hour is but the twinkling of the eye or it is nigher still.

As we position ourselves in the blossom of the new century, an uncanny sense of uncertainty, terror and hope should haunt and plague our minds.

It would certainly behoove the masses of African Americans to forget or set aside their differences and in the strength of a united African American movement bring out a new interpretation of African American plight to this unwilling world.

Following the religious teachings of their traducers, the African Americans do not show anymore common sense than a people would in permitting criminals to enact the laws and establish the procedure of the courts by which they are to be tried.

Unfortunately, the long term effects of slavery have conditioned and groomed many of us African Americans to remain locked into a comfortably familiar psychological bondage that fears and repulses freedom according to the true definition of the word.

This mode of thinking is evident in the insanity displayed during the process of our delusional movement from one level of poverty and disparity, to the very same or increased level of that same disparity, very much like "trading the witch in for the devil" and expecting different or better results.

No doubt, this illustration of insanity is a product of slavery and continual oppression and seems to have become inherently manifested in generations of African American offspring.

The final hour is the last hour in the last day and is the day that Allah (God) has decreed for man to reap what he has sown and America is reaping what she has sown and so are we.

African Americans have rejected and ignored warning and good instructions from countless great and noble leaders of the past and barely acknowledge the dreadfully obvious shouting signs of the time. Ironically, it seems that when alarms are sounded, indicating warning and danger, African Americans have begun to vicariously hit the snooze button and go back to sleep.

The African American journey of odyssey ("wandering") has been comparable to a cancer we've been fighting since coming to the shores of America as chattel slaves.

The cancer at first is detected in its early stages and as a result of ignoring its gradual progression and failing to employ treatment, it metastasized into a stage four incurable and non-treatable terminal cancer of which will certainly cause the life of the cancer victim to terminate in a very short time. This is the relentless time in which the doctor informs the patient and family that there is nothing else that they can do for the patient except, try to make the patient as comfortable and pain free as possible.

The prognosis of African American collective survival and sustainability has unequivocally become terminal, exceeding far beyond the stages of any possible remission or effective treatment. The cancer scenario described here has become an emblematic reality that African Americans repeatedly find themselves in due to their continuous epidemics of complacency.

Children represent the future of family, community or a nation, and African Americans have become distant or disconnected from the concerns and conditions of their children, the results of which caused resentment, indifference, and cold callousness to manifest itself in them.

The connectivity herein; described is the same connectivity that they attempted but failed to attract in their parents and the unison of family, they sought and found in friends, peers and gangs that welcomed and shared the same sentiments.

Their disturbing inherent resentments and anger festered against recent generations of parents who failed to ensure any significant level of socio economic prosperity towards their future by having established and maintained an African American economic tier and infrastructure that would sustain the race and provide socio economic access into the future, similar to the economic and political strategies Euro-American Caucasian Jews exercise, is in part what enables African American youth to imperviously depreciate the value of human life.

Once a human being becomes desensitized, that individual is the perfect candidate to employ for the termination of other human beings whether they be innocent bystanders or little children and babies caught in the cross fire of what has become, casual gun fights.

The resulting remorse that would be normally felt by a human being would not be experienced by a desensitized person because the hearts of these human beings and so many like them have been replaced with the animalistic heart of the beast.

This desensitization does not restrict itself to the shooter that needlessly takes the life of another human being; it trickles down into communities of Black people that have become emotionally numb and conditioned to regularly expect and accept these killings as a normalcy to their every day life.

The core of most of the issues placed before African Americans is that they have allowed themselves to be reduced to a savage and abject state. The very forces that once guided their good humane reasoning has departed them and demonic forces now guide them and their judgments against all good reason. Over a period of time, the retrogressive behavior and expressions of this type of decadent insensitivity amongst African Americans has caused our despairing social conditions to go from a flicker to a flame and ultimately an uncontrollable fire threatening to burn through centuries of African American constructive accomplishments.

There was a time when only the American white man was insensitively capable of murdering innocent human beings but it's become quite evident that that form of American cancer has also spread throughout the American body inclusively infecting the African American.

Human sensitivity is an emotion that's nurtured in the very early stages of life by family or family-like humane civil social environments that include an array of displayed affections and attention.

We have irresponsibly neglected to teach and inform our children of our recent history and our overall history of struggles and that that they learned about on their own has angered them because they can't for the life of them understand or come to grips with why most African Americans were never really vengeful towards their real and open enemies. They inherently understand that the enemy of the oppressed people is an enemy of God's, but perplexed with, why the oppressed would befriend their enemy and God's enemy knowing that there is reserved place in hell for the enemy of God to abide in forever and those who befriend the enemy will abide there with him forever.

African Americans have yet to sincerely atone for their shortcomings, acknowledge fault or express regret, even in the lateness of this final hour of which we have begun to experience reaping the recompense of our failure to provide for our children and befriending God's enemy and our enemy.

Our repetitious selling out, miss-education and minuscule esteem has left us African Americans stagnated in a funk of helplessness and shame that has yet to be addressed.

Our enslavement and oppression has caused us enormous guilt and grief, a grief that we foolishly pretend is minimal and under control, and guilt that clouds our judgment and often time's prompts ill behavior.

Grieving over the most horrific atrocity inflicted on human beings would purge our souls and hearts of much, if not all of the poisons produced by the inflictions, and the strong emotion of guilt could be reversibly used as a motivator.

The toil that has afflicted African Americans has caused our conditions to go from pitiful despair, to fatally catastrophic with the enormous increase in Black against Black violence and reduction in concern for Black life.

In 2010, before the end of the year, Newark, New Jersey has become the new poster child for Black against Black crime. Crime in Newark, New Jersey rose to severely critical heights that summoned the National Guard and the attention of African Americans throughout the country.

The crisis in Newark, New Jersey prompted concerned Black organizations and leaders to call for town hall meetings and conferences to urgently intervene and remedy the out of control murder and violence in Newark and cities throughout the country experiencing similar spikes in crime and violence rates.

On Sunday January 2, 2011, Minister Louis Farrakhan, of The Nation of Islam, was a guest on "Open Line" a Sunday morning talk show on the New York City based radio station; 98.7 Kiss FM.

The hosts of the show invited Minister Farrakhan on the show for his valuable and desperately needed input towards resolving the despairing issue of out of control violence and murder in African American communities and particularly Newark, New Jersey.

The hosts of the talk show informed Minister Farrakhan of their plan to summon all concerned residents of Newark, New Jersey and all concerned outside supporters to a forum in Newark, and then asked the minister for his remedial suggestions. Minister Farrakhan replied; "It's too late", and expressed that the situation in Newark, New Jersey was an unfortunate sign of things to come. He went on to say that political movements like the "Tea Party", was just the beginning. The awareness of this sad reality is not limited to the intuitions and perceptions of Minister Louis Farrakhan, but in recent years had already become of major concern and a common topic of discussion among many in the African American communities who also realize that the out of control violence amongst African Americans throughout the nation is symptomatic of deeper neglected issues that cannot be solved with "Town Hall-feel good sessions".

Meetings where the people in the affected communities come out get hyped up, by what they hear, and made to feel good only until the next meeting.

"It's too late" is neither a prophetic statement nor a warning; it's a dangerous reality being acted out before us in real life and time.

The warnings were already preached and announced throughout previous decades and to no avail.

"It's too late" means that expert high-tech security mercenary outfits like Blackwater USA, (a private military company founded and established in the US in 1997) training civilian police departments in locations like Los Angeles, California, with armor piercing bullets will soon be coming to a neighborhood near you to restore law and order or to assist in the implementation of martial law.

The need for African Americans to heed good instructions and cautious warnings has gone from urgently important, to absolutely imperative.

Our more than four centuries in America has been a viable developmental challenge that recently converted into a record breaking life threatening crisis.

Ironically, les than a week after Minister Louis Farrakhan, responded with those statements, a gunman in Tucson, Arizona opened fire on a crowd of people who had gathered outside of a supermarket to greet and hear Congress Woman; Gabrielle Giffords speak.

Of this attack several people either died or were injured and Mrs. Giffords was among the critically injured.

There had been several previous threats to Congress Woman Giffords life however, this time the threats had transformed into despicable realities.

It was first speculated that the recent hate fanned by the "Tea Party" regarding immigration particularly in the state of Arizona, contributed to this horrendous act of violence and later concluded that it was a mere individual act of insanity that had been festering for some time.

In fact, some of the speculation arose due to posters created by the "Tea Party"; as they had Mrs. Giffords face on a target poster detesting her support for Mexican immigration issues.

Ironically, in the state of Arizona sales for the type of gun used in the shootings rose 60% within a week and people actually stood in lines outside gun stores to purchase that same type of gun.

Minister Farrakhan has always been an exceptionally wise and inspiring man who preached hope, and was now once again compelled to inform his African American people of the painful truth of the final hour and no doubt, the Million Man March that he was credited for conceptualizing and responsible for orchestrating was an opportunity for African Americans to reverse their deteriorating conditions which they had actually indubitably begun to do.

I confirmed something from the radio dialog featuring; Minister Farrakhan that I realized for some time but hesitated to conclude, and that was simply that; Minister Louis Farrakhan had actually taken his people as far as he could take them and gave them divine warning, and good specific instructions to follow as they tread the rough treacherous road ahead.

In spite of notices of caution and good traveling instructions, African Americans once again, precipitately delved into dangerous zones of complacency that has brought us to this regretful final hour of reckoning and recompense. African Americans have unfortunately, been down so long, the thought and desire of getting up has yet to cross their minds.

Conditions of the current day are determined by the past, which for African Americans, speaks to neglected urgencies and vital importances of our past.

The repetitive downward trends make it difficult for the African American to detach the endangering modes of complacency.

I have agonized over the fact that our complacency will unfortunately and un-favorably cause us more African American community environments of intensified hazards and hostilities without contingency emergency rescue and survival plans.

I also realized that Minister Louis Farrakhan was the very last of the old school of visionary "wisdom leaders and thinker's" like Malcolm X, Martin Luther King and Elijah Muhammad. Though the African American plight has been riddled with shame, guilt and certainly the devastations of routine evil racist assault, I sense that this is truly the end of the ride for African Americans and if we are to survive the evils ahead it's going to require all the prayers we know and lots of extra hard work in the midst of very tumultuous times.

Our future advances and maneuvers for a collective beneficial progress must be made strategically and executed delicately to avoid any chances of an apocalyptic finale.

African Americans must immediately, halt their non-progressive steps, change course and execute a more effective subversive action that will benefit the entire race.

We must urgently design and implement comprehensive strategies for our survival and sustainability in the future global world movement and in our local communities.

Due to our refusal to heed warning and good direction, combined with the drudgeries of national economic crisis and what I perceive to be divine intervention and recompense, the light at the end of the tunnel has been turned off for African Americans and the journey beyond the end of the tunnel can only be accomplished by those already knowing the way despite the darkness.

While African Americans were in the midst of repairing their damages and reconstructing their communities, racist evil forces were working rapidly to un-do every one of our repairs especially those having any connection to Minister Louis Farrakhan.

Treacherous deceitful Euro-American Caucasian Jews who are the authors of conspiracy, plots of intrigue and control all the country's financial institutions, media, the vital mechanics of government and capable of strangling any economy, went with malicious intent, to the Black clergy and threatened to dismantle and dissolve their religious integrity and establishment, if they didn't immediately disconnect their association with Minister Louis Farrakhan despite any unified pending plans they might have in place for the uplift of Black people in America.

Anyone that Black people listen to poses reason for serious concern by those that viciously profit from their current demise and fear of independence.

Fear is a state of nervousness fit for children and not man. When a man fears a creature like himself he offends God.
Those spineless clergy and Black leaders reluctantly but comp licitly honored what the wicked controlling dictating Euro-American Caucasian Jews demanded of them and which consequently set the African American community further back adding insult and

un-sustainable intensity to a severely decaying situation, but reassured the former slave masters that they wouldn't be running out of fools or 21st century slaves any time soon.

This particular type of clergy member is simply characteristic of the type of people that pray to Jesus and await His second coming, but are really looking for and expecting Santa Claus.

The most distinguished virtues of great leadership are the desire, courage and ability to cut against the grain.

African Americans must demand of superficial clergy, who opt for capitulation even before considering compromise, that they stop putting the divine holy name of Jesus on things that are not Jesus stuff.

It is sad and quite unfortunate that the absolute chief opponent to total African American emancipation, justice, equality and empowerment is the African American, who has sadly been tricked into becoming his own hindrance, worst enemy and will continue to keep his own people shackled in socio-economic and psychological bondage at the disposal of the former slave master and stands no chance against the ignorance of himself.

The historically evil vicious captivity techniques used by European's to abduct and enslave Africans, which primarily entailed the "tricked" use of fellow Africans to perform the captures, is still quit prevalent amongst Black's today, though under different but very effective guises and ascertains that African American slaves are still available and for sale despite their nominal emancipation.

W.E.B. Du Bois concluded before his final departure from the United States, that "the Negro in America doesn't stand a chance", I am certain that his heart ripping statement included: African American self betrayal and sale. When oppressed people accept injustice they become unjust themselves.

African Americans continuously follow and deeply involve themselves in the dangers of conjecture. One of the behaviors commonly characteristic in the illness of insanity is; doing the same thing repetitiously, and expecting different results. The results African Americans acquire will be solely pertinent to their actions. There is for a certainty, a variable element of insanity amidst the psycho-socio behaviors of African Americans and urgently in need of repair.

Sadly, but conveniently overlooked is one of the most prolific aspects in the equation of American and world human perpetrated devastation and destruction is simplistically, that the wicked atrocities are all brought on by people who superficially profess and practice Christianity in the name of Jesus.

While the evils of people who proclaim Christianity are executed, African Americans fulfill their Christian pledge of "Love thy enemy" and "Forgive them father, for they know not what they do".

I am for certain, no religious scholar, nor a student of religious studies, but I'm quite certain that the divine prophecy and teachings of Jesus are not reflected in America's white supremacist murderous, tyrannical and imperialistic behavior.

Simplistic and very basic historical fact would cause anyone to conclude that the historical world wide murderous evils of Euro-American white Supremacy perpetrated throughout the modern world are actually executed and cloaked in the good name of Christianity and Jesus Christ.

African Americans, who consider themselves Christians, must be reminded that Jesus was not a conformist to the ways of the world, instead represented opposition to evil, injustice and all forms of worldliness and un-righteousness. Jesus emphatically insisted; "Whoever is of this world is not of me".

The holy and divine spirit of Jesus Christ would not, and cannot dwell in such evilly hostile atmospheres overflowing with conjecture.

African American people have never been taught what religion is, and most of their preachers find it easier to stimulate the superstition which develops in their unenlightened minds. Religion in such hands then becomes something which is used to take advantage of weak people. Why try to enlighten the people in such matters when superstition serves just as well for their exploitation.

African American clergy and leadership are scrambling all about the floor like abject dogs desperate to get what little discarded scraps of food the master rakes from his plate and have now forsaken the remaining minimal bits of pride and dignity acquired throughout the African American plight.

The plight, struggle and movement of African American people is now abandoned by the people who swore to their God in the name of Jesus, that they were divinely called and convicted to ride out the storms of maze and withstand the destructive winds of disparity to the very bitter end.

Ironically, most of those asinine half baked leaders and people that abandoned the plight did so before the storm arrived, in fact, they were deterred by the mere rumored threat of a storm said to be on the horizon and willfully cashed-in their own small self-worth for a minimal dollar amount. In most instances, African American Christians and Muslims practice religious rituals well, but have for far too long, neglected to contribute to their social improvement.

Many African Americans wondered what had actually happened after the Million Man March that caused the spiral downward in African American affairs. This was clearly the quiet, sneaky and vicious beginning of the un-doing of bringing millions of Black men together in spiritual and physical unison to remedy and repair the overwhelming damage done to the African American community.

After the Million Man March, African Americans once again created and acted out a stupefied hypnotic fantasy relationship with the white man, which is drastically different from what unfortunately prevails in reality. Reality presents a former slave and former slave master's, sadomasochistic, "love hate" relationship.
The former slave loves the former master, but the former master hates and abuses every aspect of the former slave's existence. These fictitious fantasy relationships have been repeated periodically throughout the odyssey and history of African Americans largely due to multiple personality disorders developed in African American people as a result of post slave syndrome. Multiple Personality disorders present typical conflict traits in African Americans.
The most common being their diligent struggle and desire to be other than who they really are.
African Americans have undoubtedly, demonstrated themselves to be the most adaptable people on earth.

However! Adaptation is not always the best thing though it is sometimes the necessary thing.

African Americans cannot sustain themselves in an "IPAD" technological world while maintaining 8 track thinking. The African American community will undoubtedly be taken to task by new world globalization and our response to such a task must not include a desire for African American men to continue amusing the world with their pants sagging and literally displaying their asses and leaving viewers to wonder if they should compliment the spectacles on the contour of their ass and choice of drawers, and not certain if the visual attention attracted is sufficient to soothe the African American male craving for attention to their immature, obscene and corrosive behavior.

The Sagging Pants trend is one of the worst aspects of the twentieth century renaissance and reflects all the African American asininities and ills of that century and carried its obscene perversity into the twenty first century. The world laughs at African Americans for throwing away the hard earned dignity that took centuries to achieve. The world was already laughing at us with contempt and pittey; because we neglected to tend to our urgent matters, but now they laugh because we confirm their negative perceptions of us with our behaviors of asinine buffoonery which is clearly symbolic in our shameless petulant display of "pants down and ass out". Young African American men are literally "doing the butt" engrossed in an ass competition which is far more intense than the way woman display their butts and has added immensely but quietly to the competition woman already had with each other. The old school version of "doing the butt" was by comparison, minute and reflected in Spike Lee's 1988 music drama movie; School Daze but has since taken on a new male ass image, sexual orientation, and practice.

"You have really shown your ass" is an old school common reprimanding statement meaning; the individual reserved no shame and instead represented a total disgrace and embarrassment to themselves and anyone witnessing their gross and rude behavior. The intensity of African American disparity results in impediments like "sagging pants".

The future of African American people cannot be viewed solely as a gift, but must also be given the sincere and respected recognition of an achievement.

African Americans must be mindful of the serious fact that slavery in America does not, and will not ever end until African Americans free themselves.

The divine mercy of Allah, the shoulders of our beloved African American ancestors and "Amazing Grace" "got us over" and to this particular point in our plight.

For a surety! The final hour won't on a morality basis, award a socio-economic promotion for African Americans without the hard work and earned achievements in those areas.

I am hopeful that the African American Odyssey will spark a stimulating desire in African Americans to segue on to the road destined to survival, sustainability, progress and redemption.

African Americans must discontinue reveling in corrosive toxicities and get back on track; resume the journey with our best course of action which is the old familiar two-pronged approach: Blending the best of our wisdom with good direction.

The portrait of the African American has quite often been drawn by the pencil of those desiring to portray the African American in a distorted context of amusing comic tragedy, destitute hopelessness, and pity.

Herein now lies the opportunity for the African American artist as a world reformer. Will he seize the opportunity and live or continue the mere imitation of others and die.

Though I maintain a skepticism born out of countless disappointments in my people, I still believe that if granted the opportunity, African Americans would choose to take better care of their socio-economic affairs.

The final hour, as limited as it may be, still provides opportunity for a last ditch effort in which the African American must develop and exercise the highest levels of competencies, become more discretionary in their choices, then redefine and readjust their plight in a synergistic manner.

FOR ALL WE KNOW, WE MAY NEVER MEET AGAIN, TOMORROW MAY NEVER COME, SO LET'S LIVE, LOVE AND ACHIEVE ALL WE CAN TODAY WHILE ALLAH SHINES HIS DIVINE LIGHT ON US.

ACKNOWLEDGEMENTS

In the most holy name of Allah, The Beneficent, The Merciful.
All praise is due to Allah, Lord, Cherisher and sustainer of all the worlds.
Thee do I worship, and Thine aid alone, do I seek.

I acknowledge direct receipt of the hard earned unlimited great benefits achieved by my African American ancestors. I believe that everyone has a debt to society; hence, the completion of the African American Odyssey is hereby submitted as a down payment on my debt to the legacy of my family, my African American people, society and the gracious universe that I am blessed to share. I have made every effort to re-adjust my thinking at the introduction of each African American renaissance that I've experienced during the tenor of my life resulting in only a few significant regrets.

The most prominent of my regrets maintains strong conviction and anxiety regarding the regretful fact that in the past recent decades African Americans have presented an inability or lack of desire to repair their torn conditions and image in the world and continue to live on the edge of society. My delight in researching and reading through the pages of our African American history is stimulated by the parts that portray African American family and community connectivity and strong unwavering will. I am still hopeful that

Allah will execute one of His limitless miracles to deliver us from despair if it be His will.

My son Bilal, whose idea it initially was to create this writing project and who during his early childhood was quite precocious, Even to this date as a mature adult man, always insist on knowing the recent and past history of his family and African people.

Because of our continuous in-depth discussions and coaxing from him, I was prompted to write some of what I know and experienced for the informative benefit of anyone that might be interested in reading my recollections.

My youngest grandson, Kasim Raqib Muhammad, shares his father's precocious characteristics and will hopefully find identitification, pride, ethnic dignity and at least some of the answers to his history in this book and regard it as an inheritance and template directing his future.

My dear and beloved grandson, Kasim,

Always remember to avoid things that are doubtful, keep your heart clean and righteous, and Allah will speak to it that you may go forward in life as an up-right progressive human being and never are you to forget your way.

My dear beloved brother Alik, AKA (Eddie Henson)

I want to extend to you from the depth of my heart; a very special thanks that I figured could be best expressed in this acknowledgement so that it could forever remain documented.

Thanks! For the confidence and admiration you've expressed in my writing projects even before they were completed.

Your enthusiasm has inspired and propelled me to keep on writing knowing that you would be waiting in the wings to read the finished product.

You and I go a ways back and it's been a delight knowing you and exchanging verbal notes with you especially on subjects and issues concerning the Knowledge of our African American history, as well as the history of all other people of the earth.

I will never forget nor be oblivious to your eagerness to support my writing projects.

You have proven to be none less than the epitome of a loyal friend, sacred brother and strong solider who has been on the battlefield fighting according to your own means, for the African American struggle for several decades and never gave up despite the at times, seemingly un-winnable odds.

Brother Karief, I've got to tell you that your spontaneous interest, support and pursuit of my writing projects made me wish I had contacted you when they first became available because your enthusiasm about them is a motivator and I hope that this book also serves to satisfy your intellect. Thanks for the support and remember you've got my support at your beckoned call and disposal.

I would like to give a special thanks and an honorable mention to Ms. Andria J. Brown, who played a very significant and pivotal behind the scenes role in the production of this book and many of my life long endeavors.

Ms. Andria J. Brown, I salute you for being a woman who has unequivocally earned and justly due the nobility and honor Allah intends for you, and I hereby, honor you for the authentic gifts that the Almighty has produced through you. Thanks for the supreme gifts we share. You should further know, that the respect I maintain in the reserve of my soul for you has been renewed with a more matured appreciation and proper perspective of things and life.

Thanks for helping to make this world a better place for humanity to dwell in.

You are the scorned and envied Black woman that I've read about in various scriptures, yet you replicate the epitome of the Royal Majestic African Queen that gives life to a nation then tries diligently to nurture its existence, then with propensity, protects and sustains the nation.

May Allah reward you!

Of all our many historic and heroically wonderful great African American leaders, the Honorable Minister Louis Farrakhan is essentially the only one left.

I am forever grateful for his non-conformity, deep, yet, superlative wisdom, dedicated efforts and the many years of hazardous demanding hard work he put into sustaining his African American people.

A man who's leadership ability is clearly embedded in his "divine chemistry" and over-all human make up.

There is clearly only one Minister Louis Farrakhan.

However! He shares a most significant part of himself with each and every one of his people of color and those White's that share his same God-given basic human principles.

I maintain the utmost respect and honor for the contributions and sacrifices made by Minister Louis Farrakhan and thank his wonderful family for all the years that they deprived themselves by sacrificing him for what they assiduously considered would be the empowering benefit of our African American people.

Some of my deepest appreciation is lastly extended in tribute to the memory, effort and hard work of my first teacher in Islam, an un-sung hero in the struggle for African American Civil Rights and Human Rights; Sheikh Daoud Ahmed Faisal who insistently taught me during my early youth, that Islam is the religion of humanity and encouraged me to work and pray towards being the very best Muslim human being possible and at the same time make every available effort to improve overall humanity as Allah would have it. It would be further accurate to state that most if not all of the African American thinkers, leaders, and pioneers of the past have been my teachers to some valuable beneficial level.

I pray to Allah, giving thanks and gratitude to Him for his guidance and assistance in the completion of this writing project which otherwise could not have been possible. The encouragement and push from my very dearly beloved son Bilal, enabled me to reach yet another production deadline. Thanks, Bilal and May Allah reward you.

I am therefore, hopefully optimistic that this book will serve to stimulate thinking and progressive action amongst African American people and may the peace and blessings of Allah be upon us and may He Allah, give renewed guidance to the little lambs that have lost their way. **Amen!**